THE
JOYS & CHALLENGES
OF FAMILY LIFE

CATHOLIC HUSBANDS AND FATHERS SPEAK OUT

THE
JOYS & CHALLENGES
OF FAMILY LIFE

CATHOLIC HUSBANDS AND FATHERS SPEAK OUT

Brandon McGinley, Editor

Our Sunday Visitor Publishing Division
Our Sunday Visitor, Inc.
Huntington, IN 46750

Copyright © 2015 by Our Sunday Visitor Publishing Division, Our Sunday Visitor, Inc. Published 2015.

20 19 18 17 16 15   1 2 3 4 5 6 7 8 9

ISBN: 978-1-61278-813-5 (Inventory No. T1619)
eISBN: 978-1-61278-373-4
LCCN: 2014959189

Cover design: John Lucas
Cover art: Veer, iStock Photos
Interior design: Dianne Nelson

PRINTED IN THE UNITED STATES OF AMERICA

Note to Reader

This book is an answer to a question that came to mind while I was in the shower, where I get most of my worthwhile ideas: What do Catholic husbands and fathers need to help us navigate the turbulent seas of modern life? Most of all, we need examples of other men who are experiencing or have experienced the same excitements, the same tensions, the same worries that we go through every day as we build our lives and our families and our relationship with God.

Admit it: You've had doubts about how you're doing as a husband and father. Am I raising my children to be able to stay strong in the faith? Is my relationship with my wife what it ought to be? Do other men share my struggles with sin and anxiety? We've all asked questions like these from time to time, but usually in the silence of our trembling hearts (yes, men's hearts tremble) during Mass, or lying down in bed at night, or in a quiet moment at the office.

This book is not a collection of simple answers to these questions (except the third, and the answer is *yes*). Rather, it is an assortment of reflections that aim to help you make sense of your own experiences and to build the family life you desire—and, more important, that God desires for you. You will find in these pages the wisdom and understanding, but also the humor and vulnerability, that come with experiencing all that Catholic family life has to offer.

Now, not every chapter might be relevant to you right now. That's fine. This is a book meant to be nibbled, not scarfed.

Feel free to skip around as your interest and your season of life changes.

My prayer is that reading the following reflections will fill you with the hope—for yourself, your family, and the world in which we live—that I felt while editing them.

—Brandon McGinley

Contents

Chapter I

New to Fatherhood:
Having it All—Rightly Understood

By Brandon McGinley

Sometimes I just want to sit at a bar with my wife, Katie, sipping a decent bourbon and eating anything fried. Sometimes I just want to hang out with friends talking about politics, sports, or even the weather. Sometimes I just want to play golf or street hockey as if I were fifteen years old again. Sometimes I just want to watch a movie—a good movie, a bad movie, any movie—in peace.

In July 2013, Katie and I welcomed our first child, Teresa Benedicta. Teresa is objectively the most attractive baby in the history of humanity, so we consider ourselves very fortunate. Next to her, the Gerber baby looks like an orc child. If I had my way, this chapter would be illustrated with pictures of her, but my editor said something about printing costs. As if you can place a price on cherubic radiance.

In all seriousness, just in trying to think of non-clichéd ways to describe my feelings for Teresa, the muscles in my face begin to loosen in that telltale precursor to tears. She's a fussy, spitty, messy, stinky angel. But, though I've never seriously wanted to return to my pre-baby life, I do very often want a break—a bit of time to cultivate the hobbies and pastimes that I enjoy without the responsibilities of caring for a helpless little one.

Just typing that sentence I feel a tinge of guilt. I can almost hear the scolding voice: "What do you mean you don't want to spend *every waking moment* with your infant daughter! You may *want* to live like a bachelor, but those days are behind you, chief. You're a dad now, and that means *everything* is *always* about the kids and *never* about you. Don't be like all those *other* men on TV who resent their kids as anchors on their social lives."

Of course, my internal scold has a point. In this age of perpetual adolescents, Catholic fathers are called in a particular way to be signs of contradiction to the most destructive aspects of our culture. We are to be devoted to our families before everything and everyone but God himself. I am not the first to point out that nothing challenges selfishness and teaches selflessness like parenthood.

But must we dads hollow out all other aspects of our lives to fulfill these duties?

CHANNELING DAD GUILT

The concept of "having it all" is a staple of discussions about women's anxieties over balancing family duties with other fulfilling aspects of life, but it's absent from men's discourse. It shouldn't be. This is especially true for young first-time dads as we try to navigate the uncharted waters of careers and hobbies complicated by children.

I want to have it all. Like other young fathers, I want to be able to care for, play with, and adore my little girl—not just because it is The Right Thing To Do, but because I love it. And, also like other young fathers, I want to do all the things I did before she burst onto the scene. Can these desires be reconciled? How can young dads lead dynamic, textured lives full of interest while still joyfully fulfilling our responsibilities to family?

There are no easy answers to these important questions, and everyone's circumstances are different. Even so, there are widely applicable ways to think about these challenges that have emerged from my experience, observations, and reflections. But first, a word about my own circumstances.

My wife and I met through the Catholic ministry at Princeton University, where we studied as undergraduates. After about a year of dating, I proposed on the shores of Lake Carnegie, a reservoir financed by the famed industrialist, just as the U.S. National Rowing team scooted past—followed by coaches on motorboats. So that moment was a bit more boisterous and public than I had anticipated.

Nevertheless, we graduated a few weeks later, in June 2010, as an engaged couple. Getting engaged on campus was a remarkable experience. Universities such as Princeton have a well-deserved reputation for hostility to the old-fashioned institution of marriage. On the one hand, intellectuals and excitable young adults wax poetic about sexual liberation. On the other hand, the materialist expectation that a degree will be parlayed into immediate financial triumph counsels against distractions like children. These two phenomena, of course, are not unrelated.

And yet the reaction to our engagement, as well as the others that tend to occur around that time, was downright ecstatic, and not even just among close friends. The congratulations we received from so many were so sincere that I couldn't help but detect a certain wistfulness in these acquaintances. Though they had been steeped in an aggressively secular culture, even the most irreligious seemed to deeply appreciate, even envy, our commitment.

It's been clear to me ever since that joyful, authentic Catholic marriages have a visceral appeal to them that cuts through the smoke screens put up by our secular culture. Such relationships are one of the most effective witnesses to the beauty and truth of Church teaching. It's difficult to buy in fully to our culture's corrosive view of marriage in the face of a walking, talking counterexample. But more about this later.

In February 2012, we were married on a chilly, drizzly, and utterly gorgeous day in Katie's hometown of Richmond, Virginia. By that Christmas we knew we were expecting our first child, who turned out to be Teresa. Like many children who emerge from NFP-practicing couples, she was neither planned nor unplanned; like all children, she just is, and that's all that matters.

We had a bout of first-time-parent panic only a few days after bringing Teresa home. An acid reflux attack looked for all the world like a seizure—writhing, foaming at the mouth, and so on. We spent a few days at the hospital while every possibility was ruled out, leaving only one blessed option remaining: perfect health. I do look forward someday to showing her the pictures I took of her tiny head covered in wired probes for a precautionary brain scan.

There's nothing that drives home the life-changing nature of parenthood like an early health scare. These events, no matter how they ultimately turn out, throw into the sharpest relief just how helpless this little human is, and just how profound our parental responsibilities are. And they strengthen the anxiety about not doing enough and the guilt that accompanies the desire for normalcy.

In a certain respect, of course, these stressful feelings are perfectly good and natural, especially for first-time fathers, and there's not much to do about them. We *should* feel and embrace that protectiveness, that drive to do anything for the good of our children. Some would argue that this is the opposite of natural, and that men's default condition is emotional aloofness to their own children in deference to the drive to procreate continuously. There's really nothing else to say: these people are vicious and should be shamed.

Making Time for God

But the competing desire for non-baby normalcy is also natural and, in its proper perspective, good. There are aspects of our continued maturation and flourishing as young men that are unrelated to child-care. (This goes for moms, too!) First and foremost are the spiritual concerns that are usually the first to be subsumed by circumstances. There is a sense in which taking care of your little one—the miraculous life created and entrusted to you by God—is a spiritual exercise. But this does not eliminate the necessity of other forms of spiritual maintenance and growth in the life of a father. I know the importance of this not because I have successfully reintegrated these important concerns into my life, but because I haven't quite figured it out yet.

As we learn how to make this all work, there are two simple spiritual exercises that Katie and I are trying to introduce into our new life as parents. First, of course, is daily prayer. It's easy (I should know) to put this off until the baby is less colicky, or until you and your spouse are both less tired, or until some other time that may never come. Don't. Even a simple triad of an Our Father, a Hail Mary, and a Glory Be allows you to carve out time for God and orient your (often frustrating and exhausting) efforts toward Him.

Second, we want to take turns watching Teresa while the other spends time at our parish adoring Our Lord in the Blessed Sacrament. We are blessed to belong to a parish that offers regular adoration; if finding such a parish is a possibility, I strongly recommend it. When we were at Princeton it was (and may still be) the only secular university in the United States to have a consecrated Blessed Sacrament Chapel within the nonsectarian university chapel. This was not adoration per se, but the experience of being in the presence of God in that space was essential to my spiritual growth in college. And it was there that I had a deeply moving, deeply personal experience that encouraged me to open myself up to the woman who would become my wife.

Remember this: adoration, like all of the above-and-beyond devotions of the Church, is not just for super-serious know-all-the-hymns bow-all-the-way-to-the-waist-before-Communion Catholics. I often fall into the trap of thinking that I'm not good enough or knowledgeable enough or experienced enough to bother making the time for adoration. This is the opposite of what I, and you, should think. The way to grow in holiness is not to sit around and wait for it to happen, but to take action.

It's no secret, though, that young dads want to do non-baby things beyond the spiritual—and we shouldn't feel bad about that, provided a proper balance is struck. In fact, I'd like to argue that we have a *responsibility* to ourselves, our children, and our communities to integrate enjoyable hobbies and activities into our lives as much as is practical.

MAKING TIME FOR YOURSELF

I've already mentioned that there are certain aspects of personal growth that aren't tied to spit-up and diaper changes. Social engagements, intellectual pursuits, athletic challenges: these are all, in different ways for different people, important parts of leading interesting and fulfilling lives. And don't forget time with your wife! It's easy to forget that the most important and available non-baby person in your life is right there all the time. If you can't find the time for a full-on dinner-and-a-movie date night, even an hour out for drinks and appetizers is often enough to satisfy that stir-craziness that sets in.

Katie and I have our best, most thoughtful and forward-thinking conversations at times like this, away from all the everyday distractions of our home—laundry, dishes, cleaning up—that get in the way of substantive discussions. It's tough to talk about plans for Teresa's education when she's fussing and there are burp cloths everywhere and the laundry's overflowing and, *crap!*, I just burned dinner.

But finding time away isn't just about personal maintenance. I am convinced that an essential aspect of parenting is modeling an appealing, joyful, interesting lifestyle to your children. My parents have always been scrupulously self-sacrificial with regard to my sister and me, and I can never thank them enough for it. But at a certain point of maturity, like most children I began to appreciate seeing my parents really enjoy themselves not just as parents, but as regular people. Part of the appeal of weekly stay-overs at Grandma's house even into high school was knowing that we were giving my parents time to themselves for a change.

The last thing we want to do as dads is signal to our kids that having children is a joyless, Sisyphean burden. Not only, of course, mustn't we suggest to our children that they are burdensome, but we mustn't portray Catholic marriage as dour. Part of bringing up our children in the faith is demonstrating that countercultural Christian witness can be energetic, happy, and, well, fun. We cannot expect our kids to want to dedicate themselves to the Catholic faith and a Catholic way of life just because we tell them to; we must, prayerfully, be appealing models of the lives we want them to lead.

Bands of Brothers
(and Sisters, Uncles, Grandparents ...)

But how, exactly, do we go about this? How do we, as new dads, actually find time for the things we enjoy? And once we find that time, how do we strike the proper balance among our responsibilities to our children, our families, and ourselves?

The cheeky answer is this: nobody knows. If there were one-size-fits-all answers to these questions, they would have been discovered and the lucky man who happened upon them would be very wealthy. Every dad has a different set of circumstances, which suggest different approaches to making it all work. In my experience and on reflection, however, there is one necessary constant that helps in every aspect of the journey: community.

By community I don't mean a commune, or your homeowners' association, or your municipal government. I'm speaking in the broadest terms. Your marriage is a community—the foundational community. Your household is a community. Your extended family is a community. Your parish is a community. Your friends are a community. All of these communities form a complex network of advice, support, and experience that makes successfully navigating the early days of fatherhood possible.

Community's most obvious usefulness is in helping to manage the logistics of a newly expanded family. There are never enough hours in the day, and fatherhood seems to contract those hours even more. Having trusted friends and family who can watch the little one expands what you're able to do with the time you have. Community support makes it possible to live something like a normal life while reminding us and the children that part of living an authentic Catholic life is participating in community and ministering to others.

Katie and I are blessed to live less than fifteen minutes away from several family members, including my parents, who have already become a huge part of Teresa's short life; these days, this is a luxury. But this side of the Badlands or the Everglades, there's always community to be found. We met one family through a Catholic young professionals group who, at that time, had four little girls, five years old and younger. During conversation over dinner they mentioned offhand that their circumstances hadn't permitted them to have a date night for over a year. So one evening Katie and I held down the fort while our new friends went to dinner. There was nothing to it: All the girls were asleep, so we just watched *Downton Abbey* for a few hours. (Though if the girls did wake up, I was very tempted to tell them we were their new parents. Bullet dodged, I suppose.)

But communities do more than make time for personal maintenance; they can help to fill that time as well. Katie is in a citywide moms' group that offers everything from book groups to field trips, and I've joined a group of young Catholic guys—mostly dads or dads-to-be—who meet for poker every month or two. It's helpful that we each have some of our own activities in addition to the things we do together. Not only does this permit us to pursue individual interests (Katie would rather undergo electroshock than gamble), but it also lessens the chance that one of us will feel unfairly burdened. Crucially, it's not about some kind of 50/50 split; rather it's about coming to understand and appreciate each other's needs for time and activities away from diaperland.

I have found the community of fellow Catholic husbands and fathers to be particularly important. The experience of fatherhood is distinct from that of motherhood, and so there are particular insights that can be candidly shared among similarly situated young men. These get-togethers are not the complain-about-your-wife bull sessions that sitcoms insist guys are supposed to have. That type of disrespectful gossip is corrosive to your relationship with your wife and the community, as it sets up the men's group as something in contrast with your marriage rather than in support of it. Personal maintenance is not escapism; it is about building an integrated life always pointed toward bringing yourself and your family closer to God. These various communities are especially important for new dads because they bring together men in different stages of life, from the elder generations in your own family to friends just beginning their own marriages. You are not alone. These men have, to varying degrees of success for sure, navigated the waters of guilt and uncertainty and fear, and they can help you do the same. And don't forget the not-quite-yet-dads in these communities. Mentoring them is an act of charity that requires you to take a step back and to reflect on your own experiences as you shift from novice to veteran dad.

These men should also be a source of accountability if personal maintenance begins to stray into a relapse of bachelorhood. A trusted friend can indicate, with a strategic glance or gentle word, that maybe it's best to pass on this last hand of poker or glass of beer. They may be able to diagnose your struggles even before you do, or to give needed perspective on issues you're wrestling with. It is a great comfort to me to know that I have several people who have my best interests at heart—that is to say, the health of my soul and the souls of my family members—with whom I can have a candid conversation if the need were to arise. This isn't idle talk: my dear friend Stephen indicated to me that, years before I knew him, his marriage nearly collapsed under the weight of his professional ambition. He credits the tough but grace-filled counsel of a mutual friend—including during a call Stephen placed while he was weeping, lying on the floor of his office—with pulling him back from the precipice. Stephen and his wife just welcomed their fourth child.

No Man Is an Island

But perhaps the most important lesson imparted by participating in the web of communities that make up our world is in the nature of those communities themselves. They aren't just networks of advice and experience, but of interdependence. Fatherhood is nothing if not humbling, and the help I've received from friends and family continually reminds me that I am not self-sufficient. I depend on my wife, first and foremost. I depend on my extended family. I depend on my friends. And they all, in different ways and to different degrees, depend on me.

These layers of dependence point to our ultimate dependence on God himself. In this world we depend on His grace—especially as made manifest in the sacraments—in every endeavor, most especially the constant battle against sin. And in the next world we depend on His mercy for any chance of spending eternity with Him. Despite the encouragements and temptations of our culture to achieve something like self-sufficiency, such radical independence is a dangerous mirage that erases not just the necessity of community, but the necessity of God's grace and mercy.

And so the question that pervades this chapter—Can new dads have it all?—comes back to God as well. If our standard of "having it all" is what our conventional culture tells us we are supposed to want—the shallow contentment that comes with satisfaction of our earthly desires—then surely we will always be disappointed. But what if instead we mean the authentic contentment that emerges from the full and fearsome experience of setting ourselves and our family on a trajectory toward paradise? Then, with work and prayer and God's grace, and in community with other men and women striving for the same, we can have it all.

* * *

BRANDON MCGINLEY writes from his hometown of Pittsburgh, where he lives with his wife, Katie, and their young daughter, Teresa. They excitedly await an addition to the family around the time this book is published. By day, Brandon works for the Pennsylvania Family Institute, a nonprofit public policy organization. By night, he writes, tries his hand at mixing cocktails, then writes some more. His work has appeared in print in *National Review*, *Fare Forward*, and the *Pittsburgh Catholic*; and online at *First Things*, *The Federalist*, *Public Discourse*, and *Acculturated*.

CHAPTER 2

Running to Win:
Cultivating the Habit of Prayer

By Daniel Stewart

KNEELING before a makeshift altar, a harrowed but focused man and woman count beads on worn rosaries. Their lips move quickly but their voices can scarcely be heard above the cries around them. Spoons and cups fly past their heads but they pray on, eyes closed, heads bent forward.

"Hail Mary, full of grace…"

A plate hits the wall and clatters to the floor.

"Blessed art thou among women and…"

The man is knocked forward by a blow to the back of the head but he doesn't stop.

"Holy Mary, Mother of God…"

A high pitched scream cuts through the air but the couple only chants their prayers louder, oblivious to the chaos around them.

"Pray for us sinners…"

Is this a scene from a new horror movie about exorcisms? Nope. It's our family Rosary time. But, with a one-year-old who lacks volume control, a two-year-old with a fondness for throwing toys, and a five-year-old who just can't help swinging his rosary around like a lasso, prayer time can sometimes feel like a strange moment from a horror movie.

I'm exaggerating here. It's not always that bad. Sometimes, we get through all five decades without any rosary-swinging accidents and with only minor screaming. And, as with most things, we're getting better as we practice. These days, my wife and I can easily comfort a crying infant, catch flying toys, and calm fidgety children without missing a bead.

As with most Catholic practices, my wife and I are learning as we go. For us, the challenge of raising a Catholic family is even more difficult because our conversion to Catholicism and the raising of our children began at the same time. We were confirmed into the Church shortly after the birth of our first child. Changing diapers was just as new as saying the Rosary. Because of this, I often wonder if I'm doing things "right." I was raised in a Christian home, so not all aspects of Catholic spirituality are completely novel. Still, I've found there are plenty of surprises.

Catholic Joy

During my brief time as a dad and a Catholic, I've experienced plenty of struggles and difficulties. But I've also experienced an abundance of grace and joy. This is true even of the structured Catholic tradition I once believed to be stifling and legalistic but have since found to instead be life-giving and joyful. I've learned to pray in a variety of ways from Eucharistic adoration to the repetitions of the Rosary to the less formal prayer I've cultivated on long, long runs. I've found the sacraments to be an invaluable source of grace without which I would fail as both a Catholic and a father.

Outside of Mass and confession, my first specifically Catholic "spiritual thing" was a weekend men's retreat at our parish. I'd been to plenty of retreats growing up, so I figured I knew the drill pretty well. This one started off predictably: talks, small groups, and minimal singing (because we're men, apparently). I was new to the parish, so I didn't know any of the other men, and I wasn't yet familiar with anyone's humor. So when several men made reference to the keg we'd tap after evening Mass, I assumed this was just an odd joke. Surely, even Catholics wouldn't actually have a keg at a retreat. But, sure enough, after an emotional day that culminated in confession, Mass, and Eucharistic adoration, we were led to the patio of the retreat center where there was a keg sitting in a trash can full of ice. Actually, there were two. One of the men leading the retreat brewed his own beer and had brought two mini-kegs filled with his home-brew. Another man brought out cigars and we spent the rest of the night drinking great beer and fellowshipping.

Now, I'm not trying to feed into the stereotype of Catholics as heavy drinkers. Not everyone there even drank. But, as I look back, I realize that this retreat set the tone for my spiritual experience as a Catholic. There was plenty of seriousness, lots of honest discussion, candor about the challenges facing Catholic fathers, and earnest resolve to live virtuously. But these things never became overly somber or dry. There was always joy, not just the pleasure of a perfectly poured beer, but true joy both in love for the sacraments and in manly fellowship.

Toward the end of that retreat we were all encouraged to join some of the men's ministries at the parish, of which there were many. The packets of information, sign-up sheets, event calendars, and brochures stacked up an inch high. Knights of Columbus, Community of Praying Husbands, Men of St. Joseph, half a dozen committees: the options were dizzying. So I didn't sign up for any of it.

The one exception was choosing a holy hour for Eucharistic adoration. Our parish is blessed to have an adoration chapel that's open twenty-four hours a day, seven days a week. Catholic men and women from all over town have signed up to be there one hour every week, even the early morning hours. For safety issues, only men can cover the hours from 10 P.M. to 6 A.M. That so many men are willing to get up in the middle of the night to pray before the Blessed Sacrament speaks volumes about our diocese. But it's also a wonderful blessing for those of us who spend an hour in stillness with Jesus.

I won't pretend that I'm always super excited to get up at 3:30 A.M. each weekend to do this. In fact, most of the time I grumble pretty loudly about it. This is especially true when we've just had a baby and sleep is the rarest of luxuries. It can be difficult to get out of bed and even more difficult to pray attentively. Nevertheless, I've had many wonderful experiences.

During the early morning hours, no one is there except for the one person signed up for the hour and Jesus in the host on the altar. I've found this hour is the perfect time to sing, yell, prostrate oneself, or pray in whatever way might not otherwise be appropriate in front of other people, which is why I'm some-times a little annoyed when someone else shows up during my time in the chapel. Occasionally a priest will come by or a doc-tor will stop in on his way home from a shift at the hospital nearby. But, for the most part, even with another person or two, the hour is still very near silence. There was one exception to this rule, though, which I stumbled upon much to my own surprise.

In the darkness of the early Sunday morning after the Easter Vigil, I pulled up to the chapel and was confused to see the parking lot and even the sides of the street completely filled with cars. I managed to find a spot and, as I approached the church, heard a large number of people singing. Just as I reached the door, there was the unmistakable sound of a tuba coming from inside. The chapel was filled with people. There must have been sixty or seventy people sitting, standing, and kneeling before the altar. And, sure enough, there were two guitarists, a man on the bongos, and a tuba providing musical accompaniment. I stood in mild shock until the man covering the adoration hour before me stood up and waved me over. He gave me his seat and then left without explaining what in the world was going on.

When the praise song everyone was singing came to an end, I leaned over and asked my neighbor, "Uh, what are y'all doing here?" He explained that they were from the local university's Catholic Student Union and that they'd gone to the Easter Vigil where several of their friends were baptized and confirmed. So they'd just stayed up all night, thrown a party, and then decided to pray and sing in the adoration chapel. Seemed like a good reason to me. So I gave up on the quiet Rosary I had planned and just enjoyed the singing and smirked every time the tuba blared. It certainly wasn't the still, almost somber reverence one might expect in such a chapel. But it was jubilant. The perfect expression of the joy of the Gospel, so near at hand on Easter morning. What better way to celebrate the Resurrection?

LIVING SEASONALLY

In general, Catholics are people who know how to celebrate. As a boy, I lived for several years in New Orleans. From my Baptist perspective, it seemed like Catholics would jump on any holiday as an opportunity to throw a party and put on a parade. At that point I didn't know anything about saints and solemnities. I just knew that Catholics got a lot of days off school. Most of my beliefs about Catholic religious and party habits were based on cultural misunderstanding. But there was some truth to my perception of Catholics as big partiers. We know how to feast.

When my wife and I first began to explore Catholicism, one of the aspects of the Church that immediately appealed to us was the liturgical calendar. We first learned about the workings and order of the liturgical year from our Baptist religion and literature professor who used to quip that the main religious holidays he grew up with were Christmas, Easter, and the Fourth of July. He was the first person to show my wife and me how rich and varied the Church year actually is. The flood of feast days and solemnities became for me a wonderful reminder of just how much we have to celebrate in Christ and the joy of the Gospel.

Now, this ought to go without saying, but there is a chasm of difference between the joyous celebrating that's appropriate for feast days and the drunken revelry usually associated with Mardi Gras that I saw in New Orleans. Real Catholic feasting is always Christ-centered and uplifting. When our family became Catholic, we began unsystematically adding feasts to our yearly routine: Michaelmas, Epiphany, the feast days of our patron saints, and the feasts of any favorite saint we happened to spy on the calendar. Since all of this tradition was unfamiliar to us, we occasionally felt overwhelmed. We researched, asked around, and guessed at the best ways to celebrate.

These days, we're still figuring things out and adjusting our lives to this calendar. However, these "interruptions" to daily routine have become joyous and life-giving celebrations for us. We have favorite recipes, drinks, and traditions for many of these occasions. Of course, the food and drink are secondary to the spiritual purpose of these feasts: to remind us constantly of the life of Christ and the saints who pursued Him wholeheartedly.

Along with the feasts, the fasts of the Christian year have been incredibly formative for me. The first year I practiced Lent I made the rookie mistake of giving up all caffeine. Still a college student, I keenly felt this sacrifice during my early classes and late-night paper-writing sessions. But, once Easter arrived, that first cup of coffee never tasted so good. The fasting of Lent served to heighten and clarify the beauty and joy of the extended Easter feast.

In many other ways, the flow of the seasons of the Church year provide a structure that helps guide my prayer, contemplation, and perspective. Moving through a season of repentance during Lent into the Easter celebration and spending a month of contemplation during Advent in preparation for Christmas—these times have become invaluable to my spiritual life. Instead of an impersonal structure of stifling legalism, the rhythm of the liturgical year has actually brought me peace and a deeper understanding of my faith.

The Church calendar is one of the many ways we tell the Gospel story. The grand narrative of this calendar is not only tremendously helpful in my own spiritual life, but also in my task of teaching the Gospel to my children. The movement from Advent to Christmas to Epiphany to Lent to Easter to Ordinary Time and then back to the beginning helps children understand the story of Jesus, our own journey as Christians, and the nature of the Church as something set apart from the culture around them. In light of this, it's difficult to see how anyone could see the liturgical year as something arbitrary and antiquated instead of lively and rich.

Similarly, in many other aspects of Catholicism, I've found that the structure and guidance the Church gives actually brings peace and freedom. Growing up in a faith that usually shunned liturgy, repetitious prayer, and tradition of any kind, this seemed counterintuitive. Yet, in the order of the Mass, the prescribed Lectionary readings, and ancient rituals and traditions of the Church, I've discovered a faith that isn't tedious but exciting and vibrant.

THE COMFORT AND FREEDOM OF STRUCTURE

I began to see the truth of this excitement in repetition when I took up the Rosary several years before converting to Catholicism. I wasn't praying the Rosary exactly "right" at that point. But the rhythm of the simple prayers was immediately comforting. Although I grew up around prayer and was raised by praying parents, I was never quite at ease with praying myself. I never felt like I knew quite what to say, and sitting down to just pray for fifteen minutes seemed nearly impossible. But the

Church, in the Rosary and in other traditional prayers, gave me the words and images—the tools I needed—to pray often and in earnest. It's such a blessing to be able to repeat the words of the Hail Mary while I think about the life of Jesus and lift up my family and other worries and concerns. In these times, I keenly feel the words of St. Paul, "we do not know how to pray as we should, but the Spirit Himself intercedes for us with groanings too deep for words" (Rom 8:26, NASB).

I'm thankful, also, that I'm able to pass down these prayers and traditions to my children. They don't fully understand these things yet. Of course, I don't fully understand them either. So we come together to pray and deepen our faith as a family. Attempting this with small children can be difficult, as I've already mentioned. But it's also of critical importance. In the midst of all of my work and time-consuming responsibilities, it can be difficult to remember, but teaching my children to pray is one of the most important things I do every day.

Additionally, the spiritual exercises I help my children practice become the foundation of my own spiritual life. We usually read the daily Mass readings in the morning and start the day off with a short time of prayer. In the evenings, we try to pray at least part of a Rosary and say a short litany of saints. Sometimes, things get in the way: burnt breakfast, escaped animals, sibling fights (who gets to say St. Michael in the litany is always a source of contention), and other facts of life. But building this habit of prayer has invigorated my own prayer life. Praying and reading Scripture with my family points my day in the right direction.

Now, despite the defense I've given for regimented prayer and spirituality, I'll admit that this kind of prayer isn't always easy for me. There's something about sitting still that I find distracting. Fortunately, there is plenty of freedom within the Church and her practices. Several years ago, I took up running. As the distance I ran became longer and longer, I found myself with lots of free time to think. This thinking often naturally turned into prayer, and I soon found that running was the perfect time to allow my mind to fall into a rhythm of repetitive prayer.

Even when running exhausts me, praying this way is always rejuvenating. I found this truth to be invaluable last year when I was seventy miles in to a one-hundred-mile trail race I'd entered. Alone in the dark on the side of a mountain, physically and mentally exhausted and practically delirious, the only thing I could think to do was pray the Hail Mary. The words had so often been on my lips while I trained that they easily came back when my mind couldn't grasp much else. This simple prayer brought comfort and strength at a difficult moment and lifted my mind out of present misery. I vividly remember watching for rocks on the trail by the weak light of my headlamp, feeling certain that I'd never make it and I would have to give up. Then, letting my mind fall back into the repetitive prayer, the despair weakened, and I knew I could finish.

Of course, the struggle of this race was something I volunteered for (some might say foolishly). But I've experienced this comfort during the more common difficulties of life: grief, loss, confusion, and trials. When spontaneous, elegant phrasing is hard coming, the simple words of memorized prayers can be a source of great relief.

The Hail Mary, Our Father, Glory Be, and other common prayers recited by Catholics do not grow stale the more they are said. In fact, the opposite is true. The meaning of the ancient words deepens for us and becomes personal and dear. Having just begun myself, I know I'm only seeing the first fruits of this.

JOURNEY OF A LIFETIME

Just as it takes time to learn to pray well, to focus, and to make the words our own, the whole Catholic spiritual journey takes a lifetime. This is part of the reason the Church so strongly encourages frequent confession and Mass attendance. The sacraments are not just a form of spiritual maintenance. They are our sources of grace, the process by which we become like Christ. There are immediate, practical benefits to spiritual discipline, of course. I find this to be especially true in my role as a father. Retreats, prayer, confession, the Eucharist; all of these things are crucial if I'm going to lead my family well. When I practice these, I'm sure my wife and children notice a man with more patience, affection, and presence of mind.

As I strive to be a better father, I often think about a passage from one of my favorite books, *Kristin Lavransdatter*, by Sigrid Undset. One of the main characters struggles with a certain temptation. He resists acting on his thoughts, but, after the birth of his son, he decides to go beyond this struggle and

34

works to transform his thoughts as well. Undset writes, "Then it was clear that he must be for Andres what his own father had been for him: a man of integrity, both in his secret thoughts and in his actions." This isn't easy to do. And it's impossible to do without the sacraments and the prompting of the Holy Spirit inside us. But as a father this is my goal: to love Christ as best I can so I can be a man of integrity for my wife and my children.

Difficult as this may be—and though I have made progress, the difficulty is still there—in pursuing this goal I have found an abundance of joy.

* * *

DANIEL STEWART is a Catholic convert who lives in the Deep South with his wife, Haley, and their three children. He spends some of his time running, some of his time gardening, and most of his time thinking about *Star Wars*. Daniel writes at daniel-bearman.com and recently published a liturgical year cookbook, *Feast! Real Food, Reflections, and Simple Living for the Christian Year.*

CHAPTER 3

More Kids? More Love:
Life in a Big Family

By Matthew Leonard

IT never gets old. A voice in the night says, "It's time." Off we go, racing through the city, praying to God there are no traffic jams. Terrifying visions of mechanical failure cloud my brain while I make every effort to speed without speeding. Maintaining calm is nearly impossible as thoughts of roadside delivery dance through the mind.

Of course, not even the parking lot guarantees safety. We once raced forty-five minutes to the hospital only to find the front doors locked. What hospital does that? I finally squeezed my wife through a door on the third floor of the parking garage. For some reason, she didn't enjoy climbing three flights of stairs during contractions.

As crazy as it is, travel to the hospital is merely the first part of the final stage of a journey that started nine months previously. Next come regular probing from nurses, the humming of computer monitors, and periodic back rubs designed to help the dad feel like he's actually doing something. Finally, it's show time. And unless you're outside smoking Lucky Strikes with the ladies who work in the hospital cafeteria, you get to witness the most amazing miracle you'll ever see—the birth of your child. All the worry and angst melt away like an ice cube in the Sahara as you behold this little person made in your image and likeness.

I've been through this process five times ... so far. And I sincerely hope to experience it again, because there is nothing like parenthood, especially when multiple children are involved. I feel sorry for people who mistakenly believe that once kids come the "good times" of marriage come to an end. This couldn't be further from the truth. Children help to solidify the marital relationship. They deepen the bond between spouses. They help turn the "good times" into "great times."

This doesn't mean you can stop working on your relationship with your wife once kids come along, though. In fact, the opposite is true.

True Love

Truly loving your spouse is perhaps the most important key in raising a family, big or small. And before you label me

"Captain Obvious," stop for a moment and reflect on modern culture.

Most people have no idea what true love is. Too often it is confused with emotion—the butterflies that tickle your stomach when you behold that other person for the first time. I'm not saying there's anything wrong with emotion, much less butterflies. Far from it. We're human and God made us to feel. I vividly remember watching my future wife descend the stairs of her parent's house on the second day I knew her. I call it "the Epiphany." Angels were singing. Palms were sweating. I was done for.

But we all know emotions come and go like a one-hit wonder. Relationships must be built on lasting love that is self-giving. What does that mean in daily life? It means taking the baby from your wife's arms when you walk through the door after work even though you're dog tired and just want to relax. It means folding all the laundry or running out to the store when the milk runs low. It might even mean (gulp) canceling your tee time when your wife isn't feeling well. True self-giving love always seeks the best for the beloved. In family life, this seeking starts with your spouse.

You can't hope to raise good children unless you're first taking care of that primary relationship. The spousal relationship is the font of sacramental grace designed to give you the love, patience, mercy, and the multitude of other blessings needed to maintain sanity while striving to raise little saints.

We're not as good about doing it as we need to be, but when Veronica and I can get out for a date night it sure helps.

It sounds facile, but it really does make a difference. We need time to focus on each other and just hang out. Of course, a lot of the time we end up talking about the kids because, other than each other, they're the most important people in our lives. What can I say? We love them! And when we're loving each other, we love them more. In fact, one of the greatest things about large families is that kids have more opportunities to learn what true love is all about. Since there are always people around, they learn to sacrifice and share. That doesn't mean the lessons are necessarily easily learned, though.

Invisible Swords

A friend of mine with eight kids once heard a terrible racket in his basement. Descending the stairs he witnessed his two young sons engaged in a heated argument that was quickly devolving into a brawl. Jumping between them like a hockey referee, he broke up the fight and demanded to know what was going on. "He took my invisible sword!" wailed the younger son. "And he won't tell me where it is!"

In order to avoid escalation of the crisis to include objects that actually exist in our dimension, my friend demanded the older son, "Go get that invisible sword and give it back to him!"

The point of the story—aside from the obvious lesson that we could all save a lot of money if we only bought invisible swords—is that brothers and sisters provide ample opportunities for expunging selfishness. There's no way around it. Kids really have to learn how to share—visible and invisible items—when the number of siblings starts to rise.

As the youngest of five kids, I somehow managed to escape sharing a room with my brothers. It wouldn't have lasted anyway. Or perhaps I should say *I* wouldn't have lasted. Older brothers apparently have a God-given ability to dream up all kinds of torture to inflict upon their little brother. Mine once tried to get me to stop sucking my thumb by putting tabasco sauce on it while I was sleeping. So I remained solo while my brothers and sisters shared rooms.

Truth be told, it kind of bums me out that I never had a family roommate. I feel like I missed out on one of the greatest benefits of large families. Because they shared such close quarters, my siblings developed deep relationships. They were buddies. And I see the same thing happening with my kids. In fact, my daughters eschew the bottom bunk and sleep head-to-toe together on the top bunk in their room. They giggle and laugh until late into the night enjoying each other's company. Having to share space in dressers (not to mention clothes) helps rid them of the "that's mine" mentality.

Don't get me wrong. My girls still argue and fight over clothes, jewelry, and who's taking up most of the covers. But they've learned to work through it and compromise. They're even learning to put the other's needs in front of their own. It's not unusual to see my oldest daughter stop her "due tomorrow" homework to help her sister work on spelling. Believe it or not, I've actually witnessed my children taking turns with what they consider to be the best seat in the minivan. And this attitude is important, because, generally speaking, visitors into your "personal space" and time don't decrease as you get older ... at least they shouldn't.

HOSPITALITY

One of the things I've noticed is that when your family is brand new you tend to protect it from other people. That was my instinct, too. Driving home from the hospital with our first baby was one of the most terrifying experiences of my life. I hunched over the wheel while furious octogenarians cast disparaging looks, blowing past me on the road. I wanted to make sure nothing and nobody brought harm to my little darling. In addition to possible road dangers, all humans represented threats of communicable diseases and were *verboten*. Visitors? "Get outta town!" Literally.

All right ... I'm exaggerating a bit. But interestingly, this insular attitude often continues to manifest itself, albeit in a different manner, as time goes by. As the brood grows, parents sometimes forget that other people even exist. Life becomes so busy with various activities that adult friends are often neglected or forgotten. My advice? Try to have people over for a visit. It's good for everybody involved. Scripture says practicing hospitality is an important part of the Christian faith (see 1 Pt 4:9; Rom 12:13) In fact, the Book of Hebrews says by inviting people into their home, "some have entertained angels unawares" (13:2, RSVCE). Time to bring out the good silver!

I know it can seem a bit overwhelming at times because there is so much going on. But my wife and I have found that when we actually get up the gumption to host another family at our house, it's generally an enriching experience. It doesn't even matter what you serve. I once made the error of attempting to grill pork chops using a brand-new electronic meat fork from which I forgot to remove the plastic tips. "Well done" doesn't even begin to describe the outcome. But we had a great time anyway, crunching through our meal. We still laugh about it today. Plus, there's a silver lining to every visit from outsiders—it's one of the few times the house gets really clean.

MESSY BUSINESS

I live in a sea of plastic. Odds are high a miniature monster or Barbie doll will cause podiatric angst in my bleary-eyed journey to the bathroom in the middle of the night. Somehow we have accumulated more stuff than should be allowed by canon law. Regardless, I've gradually come to realize a bit of domestic mess and chaos isn't the end of the world.

Many men are afraid they'll lose their personal lives, or at least their minds, if they have more than one or two kids. But life doesn't become exponentially harder once you have three (or more) children. It just means you change your defense from man-to-man to a zone. Of course, even a zone can get chaotic.

My wife often has to remind me not to make "Clean this house before I go postal!" the first thing I bark upon returning home from work. So I try to greet every child, kiss my wife, and *then* demand a bit of pickup. After all, I don't want to forget the color of the carpet.

I sometimes tell myself that one day these kids are not going to be living in my house. But to be honest, it doesn't work, because that day is going to break my heart. Every time we have a baby, I sadly wonder, "Is this the last time?" I can't imagine not having the chaos, noise, and mess in my life. As much as I enjoy a clean house, I would rather my children become hoarders than rush the day they walk out the door. (Don't EVER tell them I said that.) This is the greatest time in my life, and I have to keep reminding myself not to let messiness tarnish the experience.

The chaos around the house is just one reflection of the messiness kids bring to our lives. Our schedules fill up and get mixed up. Our attention is divided in more directions than we can possibly split it. But it all doesn't happen at once. It's a gradual process that dads of growing families adapt to over time. You get used to it, and you figure out how to carve out some time for yourself as well.

I guess one of my biggest pieces of advice for parents like me is to just relax. Do what's needed to keep the chaos at a livable level, but enjoy the moment. I sincerely wish I could take back every time I focused on the state of my environment to the detriment of my kids. I suppose it's just another in the long list of mistakes I've made. That's another important lesson I've learned over the years—you're going to screw up, but your kids will survive.

Become a Realist

The only perfect family is the divine family. And anyone with more than one child no longer suffers from delusions their kid is perfect. Remember your first? Almost every father of a son has at some point pointed out to his buddies, "Boy's got an arm, doesn't he?"

By the second child we've realized our babies probably won't be NFL quarterbacks or inhabit the Oval Office. (Thank goodness.) We're ecstatic when they can actually find their shoes without help. Some days I would settle for a child who lifts the lid. What can I say? My bar has been lowered. That doesn't mean I'm not hopeful about my children's future, but I've learned to be realistic.

Keeping it real means remembering that your kids are human. As such, they're going to do things that drive you out of your mind ... a lot! If I had a nickel for every time I exclaimed "What were you thinking?" to my kids, I wouldn't have to worry about how to pay for college. I suppose I should be grateful most of my children's moments of madness aren't exposed to the public. That's not always the case, you know.

Before Veronica and I had children, one evening we were at a colleague's house for dinner. Both the host couple and some other friends had multiple children. For reasons unbeknownst to me at the time, they decided to have the children eat first so the adults could have a bit of peace. (I have utilized this age-old technique on many occasions since.) Alas, their efforts were in vain. About halfway through the meal, a stark naked five-year-old boy came streaking through the kitchen giggling uncontrollably. Not far behind, a gaggle of children followed, shrieking and laughing. I was stunned. My wife was stunned. Remarkably, the mother of the child never even looked up. "He's only twenty-five percent civilized," she explained while poking through her salad.

Your children will embarrass you. And it's a simple equation. The more kids you have, the more times you'll be embarrassed. On the flip side, the more car seats in your van, the more opportunities for love and laughter you'll have.

I remember wondering how in the world I could possibly love a second child as much as I loved my first little princess. But when my second princess arrived, I found my heart expanded beyond any capacity I had ever imagined. And it keeps expanding. As each new addition to the family is passed to me to hold for the first time in the delivery room, I discover new depths of love. But I'm also once again reminded of the incredible responsibility put upon me by this gift from God. At the end of the day, our job isn't only to raise well-educated, well-adjusted contributors to society. It's to raise saints. Which means parents need to lead by example.

Lead by Example

Kids notice everything. Even when you think they're not looking, they are. There are lots of things we'd rather they didn't notice, of course. The world is constantly assaulting them with a barrage of evil images and twisted ideas of what life is all about. But since kids pick up on everything, use it to your advantage (and theirs). Don't hide your faith.

I made a decision a long time ago to make sure prayer is part of my daily life. Because our schedule is so chaotic, how that materializes changes all the time. Sometimes I'm able to get to an adoration chapel while other times I pray at my bed, or maybe next to the couch, or the dog, or wherever. I know I need to converse with God if I'm going to grow in my relationship with him, so I take every opportunity available.

What I didn't realize is that one of my daughters was paying particular attention to my habits. One day my wife noticed that in her diary she wrote, "Dad is my hero because when I wake up in the morning I see him praying."

You can't imagine how happy I was after hearing that. It encouraged me to pray not only behind closed doors or when the kids are asleep, but also when they might notice. I realized once again they will imitate what they see their parents doing, which puts a little bit of pressure on how we spend our time, not to mention what we say and do. The whole family is watching.

The Divine Family

Have you ever asked yourself where families come from? Here you are reading a book about parenting and family life. Why? How did this whole family thing start to begin with?

We live and love in families because it's the best way we

imitate God. The riddle of family life is solved with the realization that God *is* family. St. John Paul II once declared, "God in his deepest mystery is not a solitude, but a family because he has within himself Fatherhood, Sonship, and the essence of the family which is love."[1] This divine family is the family we were made for.

The whole reason we exist in families on earth is because we are ultimately made for family life in heaven. That's why Scripture repeatedly calls us "sons" and "daughters" of God. This isn't metaphorical language. This is reality. Heavenly life is family life. But this kind of living isn't just for later. The relationship of the Divine Family is a blueprint for how we're to live now.

As a community of persons, the Divine Family give of themselves one to another in complete self-donation. Father gives himself to Son. Son gives Hhmself to Father, and from this mutual self-donation proceeds a third Person—the Holy Spirit. In other words, all the members of the Trinity are life-giving lovers. And we imitate this relationship in our family life on earth. Husband gives of himself to wife. Wife gives of herself to husband. And from this mutual self-gift, this mutual love, comes a third person—a baby. In having children we're imaging the life of God. In other words, it makes us like God, which is our ultimate goal.

While trying to image the family of God may seem more difficult as more rug rats enter the picture, don't forget that God—our perfect Father—is always showering us with enough grace to lead our families through not just this life, but into eternity. So enjoy the kids God gives you. Revel in them. Even the ones who still can't find their shoes.

* * *

MATTHEW LEONARD is an internationally known speaker and the author of *Louder than Words: The Art of Living as a Catholic* and *Prayer Works: Getting a Grip on Catholic Spirituality*. He earned his master's degree in theology from Franciscan University. Matthew and his wife, Veronica, make their home in Ohio. More information about Matt can be found at www. matthewsleonard.com.

CHAPTER 4

Techno-Dad: The Wired Family— A Foot in Each World

By Thomas L. McDonald

I REMEMBER things. I remember being a boy.

The television had seven channels and no remote, and it stopped broadcasting around 1 A.M. If the neighbors used their ham radio, it interfered with our signal and we couldn't watch anything, no matter how much we played with the rabbit ears on top of the set. If I wanted see a movie, I went to the theater or checked the TV listings in the newspaper.

During the summer I left the house in the morning and came back at twilight—or when my parents rang the dinner bell, a sound that carried through most of the neighborhood. We wandered the woods and built bike ramps and forts out of junk lumber bristling with rusty nails. Our games were made of cardboard, and our toys had sharp edges. Our idea of high-tech was a calculator or maybe a toy that made noise at the push of a button.

There was one phone in the kitchen with a rotary dial and a cord that got tangled on itself. If I wanted to listen to music, I checked a vinyl record out of the library and listened to it on a hi-fi that glowed and hummed and gave off that slight odor of old electronics that no one will ever smell again.

And then it all began to change—gradually at first, and then faster and faster.

The phone got buttons and lost its wires. Eventually, it left the house completely and entered my pocket.

The TV grew extra appendages: a VCR roughly the size of a Dodge Dart, clicking and banging as its heads engaged the thin ribbon of tape; a cable box, complete with a large push-button remote tethered with a long, slender cable; and, finally, an Atari 2600, complete with Combat, Pac-Man, and, yes, ET: The Game. There was even a store where you could rent movies to watch. At home! Whenever you wanted!

Personal cassette players and then CDs made music more portable and clearer. The built-in hi-fi hummed no more. The smell vanished forever.

When the first kid came to school with a Casio calculator watch, he might as well have been James Bond.

The typewriter sprouted wires and was able to let you back-space to erase letters. And then the computers started coming. The first was a TI-99, followed by a Commodore 64, a Mag-navox VideoWRITER, and, finally, in college, a Northgate 8088.

Things changed, and childhood would never be the same. As much as we may mourn what was lost, we cannot un-ring that bell. But we can learn to be Catholic fathers who navigate this new world with caution and faith.

I came of age at the precise point when Then became Now, and I learned not to fear that Now. Respect, yes: like the Boy Scout is trained to respect fire while he learns to control and harness it, with eyes wide open and no fear.

THE CHILDHOOD OF NOW

My children do not wander the neighborhood. A constant drone of paranoia settled over American parents in the wake of Etan Patz and Adam Walsh and faces on milk cartons, and it never lifted. It's not a rational fear, but in fatherhood the dark rooms of the psyche open wide and appear ever-ready to swallow our beloved children whole. These monsters of the imagination don't need to be real in the material world: they are real in their essence, and that is real enough.

The free-range childhood has yielded to the wired childhood, simultaneously safer and more dangerous. My children do not gather with their friends as often as we did, and they are never far from adult supervision. They'll text and e-mail their peers, or connect via computer for multiplayer online gaming. We sat on the curb trading bubble-gum cards. They sit at home trading memes. Is one better than the other?

On any given day one of my children may be using a tablet or mobile device to read a book, play a game, write a story, draw a picture, or contact a friend. They may find themselves searching a subject in the largest library of information (and misinformation) humanity has ever known; connecting with people who share the same interests (a movie, a book, a hobby) and trials (in our case, autism and scoliosis); playing games in virtual worlds of intricacy and wonder; finding almost any song, television show, or film within seconds.

A raging torrent of pure data can now be harnessed by the smallest child. The most pressing question for a father is how to tame that torrent. Is it like a flowing river of clear, pure water, or a burning river of raw sewage? Will it nourish our children, or poison them?

Two questions must be asked when considering change of any kind: *What is gained? What is lost?* We balance gains against losses. Life does not stand still, but neither (contrary to the fundamental error of the Enlightenment) does it follow a linear progression. As the author G. K. Chesterton observed, the world does not get steadily better or worse: it merely wobbles. Life is a seesaw, not a ladder.

THE GEEK DAD

Before we turn to the challenges faced by dads in the technological age, we should consider a basic question: What is a "Geek Dad," and is it a reasonable Catholic model of manhood?

In the past, socially awkward, bookish, nonathletic sorts with unconventional interests tended to be relegated to beta-male status. In the hierarchy of manliness, the nerds and geeks who were better at coding in C++ than running a mile, or who preferred video games to team sports, were something less than the ideal.

Much of this has to do with the physical and social criteria associated with classical maleness: the male as head of the house, preferably muscular, comfortable in the company of men, and interested in conventionally manly pursuits.

No one expects this to be the default state of a modern male. In many ways, with the ascent of geek culture in the media, the hierarchy seems, at times, inverted. The rise of technology had a huge part to play in this. A figure like Bill Gates is no longer a punch line. As the joke goes, "What does a high school jock call a nerd after they both become adults? Boss."

I was never that classical male, whatever that might be. Whatever gene men are born with that makes them passionate about or even mildly interested in athletics and other activities typically associated with masculinity, I was born without it.

I am the least sporty person you'll ever meet. I've never watched an entire football, hockey, soccer, or major league base-ball game, ever. But as a young man, I had a bit of a problem. Despite my aversion to sports and my preference for books and gadgets, I happen to be just shy of six feet five inches tall, and have been since my teen years. Playing basketball was never even presented as an option. I was playing, and that was that, despite being truly awful at it.

When my knees finally went bad in high school, I was almost glad, since it meant I could quit. I was happier reading pulp fiction, tinkering with films, and writing.

When my son was born, I had to make a choice: What model of manhood would I present to him? I couldn't change myself. I was no more interested in football, hunting, or hanging out with the guys than I had been in my youth, but I wanted him to know the full range of options open to him.

And so I did what a dad should always do. I taught him how to play catch, hit a baseball, throw a football, and sink a basket the best I could. I signed him up for peewee sports and encouraged him (without forcing him) to pursue traditional team sports. I did my best not to pass my bias on to him.

By a very young age it was clear he hated it as much as I had. Comics, stories, games, and tinkering with things were his passion. He enjoyed Boy Scouts for a time because it let him shoot guns and bows and be outside, but even that eventually yielded to more technological pleasures: playing and making games, learning to code, researching his favorite things on the Internet.

Is it a fair and reasonable model of maleness? It certainly can be. A man is not a set of things he does. Maleness is our nature. In our persons, male and female share a common yearning for God and are required "to love good and avoid evil" (*Gaudium et Spes*, 16). We share a common humanity, but each sex is a different way of expressing that humanity.

Beyond his complementarity to woman, and the traditional roles of provider, protector, and head of household, the

Church and Scripture do not lay out any particular qualities for a male to "be" male. If our tendency to physical strength and action draws many men to certain pursuits, it does not mean that those things are integral to maleness.

One thing is essential for a man to be a man: his willingness to pour out his life in love for another. In this way, he models Christ. This is our essential duty. All our notions of honor, dignity, respect, and duty orbit around this core mission. This is what we are called to.

If, in their lives, some are also called to Monday Night Football while others would rather play a round of Halo on the Xbox, this is incidental to their masculinity.

This leads naturally to the basic question of how to approach fatherhood in a technology-saturated culture. Catholic families really only have two options: either opt out of the media culture completely, or attempt to let only the good things get through. Neither choice is foolproof. We live in this modern society, and opting out of electronic media—movies, television, games, music, cellphones, computers, and the Internet—is not merely challenging: it's probably unhealthy. For better or worse, this is a wired world, and our kids need some basic orienteering skills if they're going to navigate it.

DISCERNMENT

Digital technology is a medium: a means for conveying information from one source to another, whether that information is banking data, a call to a friend, research for a project, or entertainment. The volume of this data stream has reached a level unprecedented in human history. More information about more people and more aspects of life is being passed around by various technologies than ever before.

If we imagine a library as a calm and peaceful creek gently flowing with information and entertainment, we can think of the modern data stream as raging Class 5 rapids polluted with toxic sludge and beset on all sides by enemies firing upon us.

Yet these rapids are not Class 6; they are not impassable. And although shot through with sludge, there are pools of limpid calm where we can take our rest and even grow in faith and wisdom.

How do we steer toward those pools? If I had a perfect answer I'd be a happier man, but there are ways to understand the technology flow and be wise travelers in hostile waters.

That peaceful library has a defining quality: the information in it may be wrong or right, wise or stupid, but at least it had passed through many hands and numerous gatekeepers to arrive at the shelf.

The information age shattered that process, for both good and ill. Information was freed, and marginal voices could make themselves heard. A powerful elite minority could no longer control or manipulate the flow of information quite as easily. People could connect in ways never before possible.

For many Catholics, it has allowed us to share and strengthen our faith by contact with a widespread network of fellow believers through social media, online publications, distance education, and blogs.

At the same time, it flooded the zone with misinformation, hate, violence, and pornography. Dialogue among people with different views became more possible, but also more challenging, as the distancing effect of technology rendered our interlocutors faceless and thus more easily dehumanized.

In this, as in all actions, the Christian must do his best to discern the will of God, aided by Scripture, Tradition, and the sacraments of the Church. St. Paul offers clear and concise guidance: test everything; hold on to what is good.

In the information age, every person isn't capable of testing every thing because, well, there are just so many things. But you know what else is out there in great numbers? Christians, both Catholics and our separated brethren. The community of believers, and even the secular world, has an essential role to play in helping us discern the good and the bad in the realm of technology.

We're not alone in this. Not only do we have the great cloud of witnesses to aid us with their example, but the great cloud of believers. Many others are traveling this same road and have already passed destinations which remain in the distance for us. And they have earned hard-won wisdom from their experience.

That's why Catholic fathers who intend to engage the culture and the technology of our times must build a strong network of trusted guides, from local communities such as parish prayer groups, to the digital communities of social media. With a good network of like-minded men, asking a question on Twitter or Facebook about the appropriateness of a game, movie, or device will yield answers from people of faith who have knowledge and experience.

Furthermore, even the secular realm realizes the need for parental guidance. The Internet is full of sites that outline the content of any kind of media your child may request or encounter. IMDB.com has a Parents' Guide listing the violent, sexual, and language content for each film. The Entertainment Software Ratings Board (ESRB.com) rates each game from "E" for Everyone up to "AO" for Adult Only, and their site includes additional descriptions of almost all content that might be of concern for parents. Both these aids come from a secular perspective and so rarely tackle the deeper moral or thematic concerns of Catholics, but they provide a starting point for discernment.

Finally, as adult men, we have gifts which, with prayer, should allow us to discern the right path for ourselves and our families. Wisdom, understanding, knowledge, fortitude, piety, counsel, and fear of the Lord were gifts of the Spirit opened to us at confirmation. We have, within us, the ability to be guided by these gifts if we only take the time to pray and try to think with God and the deep wisdom of the Church. Coupled with plain old common sense, we can navigate our rapids with a clear eye, the collective wisdom of the Church, and the grace of God.

Laying Down the Rules

Let's look at one example. A thirteen-year-old daughter asks for a smart phone. The first step is to ask those two central questions: What is gained? What is lost?

The child will argue that all the other kids have one. She needs one to call for a pickup after practice. She wants to keep in touch with her friends. She wants to play Angry Birds. She wants to text and to talk.

Some of these points are reasonable, some not. In our house, the children know that we're just not like all the other families, so the "everyone has one" argument never even begins. We live intentionally, at right angles to society, taking the good and leaving the bad.

The image of a young person in public with her head down, shutting out the world as she peers into a device is enough to give a dad the chills. It's not a pleasant sight, but what does it mean? What is the child doing with the device?

Most likely, she's either messaging a friend or playing a game, or both. Staying in contact with others and entertaining oneself only become problems at the extremes. Thus simple rules—no devices during any meals, no devices during family time—allow you to put up limits while still letting the child have a device that provides communication, information, and entertainment.

In our house, we solved the problem simply. The kids have devices without phones (iTouch, iPad, Nintendo DS) and we have one shared phone which either child can use when he needs a pickup or she's at a friend's house. Older children may, in time, be able to earn their own phone, but no child really needs a device.

The same reasoning follows when choosing whether or not to allow kids to play video or computer games. A rough rule of thumb is: if you wouldn't let them see something in a film they probably shouldn't be experiencing a semi-realistic depiction of that same thing in a game. Additionally, games are more difficult to discern because the subjectivity of the experience—in an action game, you are doing the killing—brings the act closer to the user.

As with anything else, games must be managed. Titles must be cleared by parents. Time has to be controlled and limited. Kids should have to "earn" their time with, for instance, a comparable amount of reading or chores. They should always ask permission before beginning and agree to get off when their time is up.

Sit down, play with your kids, find out what they're doing and seeing. There are plenty of games with split-screen options—particularly the long-running Lego series—that allow a parent and child to play cooperatively for a common goal.

As for violence in games, it's a complex issue not easily settled. There is no direct connection between acts of violence in games and real violence. This is easy to prove: crime rates plummeted as the violent games became ubiquitous. However, common sense should tell us that too steady a diet of casual violence is not the ideal. One of the few definitive studies suggests violent games might coincide with a rise in antisocial behavior. At the same time, the study suggests that children who don't game are less well-socialized than those who do.

Parents may see games as a mind-sucking waste of time that turns normal people into button-pushing zombies, but for kids they are a challenge, a bonding opportunity, and a topic of discussion. In contrast to the passivity of watching television, gaming is active, putting the user in control of how events unfold through exploration, interaction, and problem-solving. Like any other media, some games are good and some are bad. And while we often talk about violent games because they are of the greatest concern, it's important to remember that the majority of games are completely benign: sports, racing, strategy, puzzle, music, and arcade games far outnumber those with violent content.

In the stormy world of adolescence, games may actually play a number of important roles, providing socialization, mental stimulation, contained fantasy, and catharsis. Making the right choices for each child at each stage in their life, however, is challenging. In the end, there's no substitute for engaged parenting.

FINDING BALANCE

Maintaining the proper balance when engaging technology can be tough even for an adult. Left to its own devices it can take over and become alienating rather than connecting, addicting rather than liberating.

Never before in history have so many people communicated with one another so much. The problem is that the people we encounter in the virtual space are proxies for reality. An e-mail exchange with a friend is a step removed from a phone call, which is a step removed from a conversation in person.

That's not bad in itself. We may communicate more if we can dash off a quick text, which really is not so different from a telegram in the early days of electronic communication.

Modern communication has its downside, however, as anyone who has ever witnessed an Internet debate knows. It provides an anonymity that allows and often encourages people to see others as less than fully human. The limitations of text preclude the finesse of conversation, where tone and posture and mere presence can add subtle inflections to even the most controversial discussions.

Technological alienation doesn't merely emerge from the limits of communication, but also from the ubiquity of technology itself. We can chart a century-long movement of technology in the home—radio, television, videotape, video games, Internet, and mobile devices—shifting the focus from the family entertaining itself in collaboration and communion with others, to a focus directed outward, onto an electronic device apart from the individual and family.

That doesn't have to be a bad thing. People can share time with a good movie or playing a game together—these things are not inherently individualistic. Indeed, the current generation of young people watches far less television than did prior generations, instead choosing forms of entertainment that are less passive and more deliberate.

But still, the risk remains that family and the community become atomized, with each person in a solitary closed loop of himself and technology. The solution is fairly simple: open the loop. Through social gaming and applications, you can use the media along with others. Choose a family digital detox day in which no electronics are used. Be intentional: make choices to use technology rather than be used by it.

Technology and technological progress, despite what our culture might lead us to believe, are not the end for which we strive; rather they are a means to our proper end: resting in God for eternity. Technology is a tool, nothing more.

It's possible for technology to serve this purpose while making our lives here on earth more fulfilling and enjoyable. It's also possible for technology to run out of control and damage our well-being through alienation from others, easy access to near occasions of sin, and the tendency of communication media to reduce our sense that a human being is at the other end of the line.

Prayerful consciousness of these problems goes a long way toward solving them, but we must always remember that if a technology does not serve the human person, its role in our lives must be reconsidered. Humanity's ability to create new technologies is a God-given gift, but like any gift it can become disordered. Just like the pleasure of sex has been severed from its rightful place in a marriage open to life, so can our talent to create and invent be severed from its purpose of serving humanity. It can become an end in itself as we push into new realms of innovation not out of need but simply because we can.

When this happens, we wind up serving technology rather than the other way around. Just as the modern man has become a slave to his sexual desire, so too may he become a slave to his technology. This is the fine line we must walk, with clear heads, a life of prayer, and a strong sense of our rightly ordered purpose.

* * *

THOMAS L. MCDONALD has been a full-time freelance writer and editor since 1991. Much of his career has been spent as a technology journalist, but for the past eight years he has also been a religion writer, contributing stories and reviews to the *National Catholic Register, Catholic News Service, Catholic World Report,* and *Our Sunday Visitor.* He earned a BFA from New York University, has a master's degree in theology with a concentration in church history, and is a catechist for the Diocese of Trenton.

CHAPTER 5

Little Apocalypses:
NFP, Risk, and Revelation

By Brandon McGinley

W HEN I was in college, a friend asked me how many children I wanted to have someday. Being the type of person who has always looked forward to having a family of my own, it was a question I had thought about before. "Two, maybe three," I answered. "One is lonely, but more than three seems unmanageable."

This conversation happened at a time when I was on the cusp of rediscovering the Catholic faith of my childhood. I had always self-identified as Catholic—kind of like the way I self-identify as a Pittsburgh Penguins fan, but with even fewer practical consequences. (I actually made time for hockey's two-and-a-half-hour frigid "liturgies.") And so, in considering the question of my future family I was drawing not from the Church's font of wisdom (of which I was only vaguely aware), but from the trough of ill-considered platitudes offered by our culture.

The interesting thing about my answer is not the number—two or three are perfectly fine numbers of children—but that I was willing to offer a specific answer with such confidence. The spacing and number of children, our culture teaches, is one of the many things over which we have (or should have) total control. From our smartphones to our meals ("Have It Your Way"), we are a culture that craves control and fears chance, risk, and helplessness.

We see this lust for control in particular, in fact, in the way our culture talks about children. We speak the words "unplanned pregnancy" in whispers, as if we're naming a fearsome pathogen. Parents label their children "planned" and "unplanned" in discussions with friends as if this is a relevant distinction. It is socially acceptable, and therefore not uncommon, for people to mention casually that they have more kids than they planned (or even wanted) to have.

The cultural message is clear: children are supposed to be planned. Planned children are to be the rule; unplanned ones the unfortunate exceptions. Not to plan one's family with precision is considered to be at best weird, at worst irresponsible. We are a culture of control freaks, all the way to trying to perfectly control the transmission of life itself.

"But wait!" I can hear you saying. "This chapter is about Natural Family *Planning*. Isn't the whole point to harness our knowledge of fertility to, well, *plan* our families?" Quite right. This chapter is *not* about what some call a "providentialist" approach to growing the family, in which fertility is not charted and the chips fall where they may. But it also is not about taking control—because we can never be totally in control, and because to expect such control from NFP or from anything in life is, always, to court disappointment and disillusionment.

More than Sex

Now, every discussion of NFP must begin with a caveat: everybody's experience is different. No two couples have the same story to tell. Some couples *are* able to plan their families very precisely with NFP, and that's great. (Our NFP instructors were kind and holy people who claim to know the exact conception date for each of their many children.) Most couples struggle in some way or another, whether with charting or periodic abstinence or discerning whether delaying conception is appropriate.

There is no one-size-fits-all solution to these often complex challenges. That's not how NFP works. Though it's based in science, practicing NFP is not scientific. It's about much more than temperatures and mucus and charts and sex. My wife doesn't practice NFP only when she's taking her temperature. I don't practice NFP only when coyly asking what day we're at on the chart (yes, I do lose track sometimes). We are practicing NFP together, all the time, and have been from the moment we exchanged vows on a rainy winter day in Richmond, Virginia. NFP is a way of life.

Specifically, NFP is a way of life that is uniquely suited to the relationship of husband and wife. Marriage is difficult. People change; needs and desires change; emotional states change; finances change; and, most of all, feelings of affection change. Our culture looks at these facts and despairs that lifelong commitment is unrealistic, and maybe impossible. As Catholics, though, we know marriage isn't impossible; nothing God asks of us is impossible. So we ask: What is the culture getting wrong? What is it not seeing about marriage?

Our culture despairs because it cannot conceive of the possibility of sacrificial love. The only love our culture considers is the feeling of romantic affection. But as even the most annoyingly lovey-dovey couple knows, those feelings wax and wane over the course of a marriage; they are unsuitable ground on which to build a lifelong relationship. No wonder marriage's stock has fallen.

Real love, on the other hand—love that honestly desires and acts toward the good of others—is a choice. Further, it is not a one-time choice, but an every-moment-of-every-day choice. That is to say, like any virtue, it is a habit. NFP helps to build the habits of self-giving love by acclimating us to thinking outside ourselves. In requiring periodic abstinence, it is a reminder that our desires are to be subservient to greater goods, including the good of others in the family. In its openness to life, it orients the mind always to our present duties, and to those future duties God may have in store for us.

In this way, not despite but *because of* the difficulty of NFP, the practice contributes to a healthy, strong, loving marriage. You know that marriage is difficult, but also that the rewards far outstrip the challenges—and are themselves fruits of successfully navigating the challenges. The same goes for NFP.

Sharing the Burden

You can't do NFP by yourself. Your wife can take a pill every day; you can slip on a condom; but you both need to participate to make NFP work. You need to discuss the time of the month and if it's time to try to conceive. You need to help each other if abstinence is proving to be difficult. You need to communicate about everything from life plans to cervical mucus.

NFP is a constant invitation to remember that the universe—and even the household—does not revolve around you. Most obviously, NFP places your most urgent desires at the mercy of someone else's bodily calendar. To make matters worse, her schedule can sometimes be just as mysterious to her as it is to you. This is a recipe for frustration.

Nothing makes frustration grow like dwelling on it. It's easy, at least for me, to enjoy wallowing in self-pity. Trust me: it's not worth it. Actually taking action to mitigate frustration voids my license to feel bad for myself.

It sounds clichéd, but it's true: look at these moments as opportunities for growth—yes, spiritual growth, but also growth in your relationship with your wife. There's no need to lock yourselves in separate rooms. Helpful, marriage-strengthening distractions include watching a (carefully selected) movie, inviting friends over, getting out for a simple date night, or even just having a substantive conversation. And remember: a sense of humor never hurts. If we can't laugh about sex, what can we laugh about?

NFP can, with our cooperation, turn our gaze away from the self in other ways. Talk with trusted friends and family about your difficulties. In the same way NFP reminds us of the importance of the spiritual support of our wives (and our support of them), it reminds us of the importance of the spiritual support of the community (and our support of our Catholic community). NFP is humbling, and that's a good thing.

Lastly, if the frustrations of NFP are growing, or if discernment of the proper moment for children has reached a standstill (a witty friend has warned against seeking the intercession of "Our Lady of Perpetual Discernment"), speak with a trusted spiritual director. That may be your parish priest, a priest or consecrated religious friend, or perhaps even a priest from your past (many of my friends still seek the guidance of their college pastors). You want someone whom you trust and who knows you well enough that you can be honest about the state of your emotional, spiritual, and, yes, sexual life.

NFP poses its greatest challenges to you and your marriage when you try to remain in control; it bears its greatest fruits when you relinquish that control to others—and to God.

"LITTLE APOCALYPSES"

In a talk at a pro-life conference at Yale University, my friend Tristyn Bloom argued that our culture's obsession with control and fear of risk fuels the demand for abortion. Unplanned pregnancies, for the single, but also for the married, explode our plans for ourselves—what Bruce Springsteen often calls our "dream of life"—leaving us unable to see a way forward.

Bloom called these unexpected moments "little apocalypses." It turns out, according to Bloom, that the word "apocalypse" doesn't really refer to destruction, but rather it comes from the Greek for "uncover" or "reveal." An apocalypse, then, is a revelation—at the end of the world, of God's plan for the universe; in our lives, of God's plan for us.

We all have little apocalypses in our lives—moments when we must toss aside our plans and accept a new reality that has been imposed on us—whether they are financial, social, or spiritual, or have pairs of arms and legs and a squashy face. NFP does not automatically make us more understanding of these moments; it is not magical. But by ensuring we are always open to life, it does invite us to be open to God's providence. It is up to us, as always, to accept the invitation.

Six or seven months into our marriage, my wife, Katie, and I began to seriously discuss if the time was right to start trying to conceive. The Church's guidance on what constitutes a proper reason to delay childbearing is, well, vague, and as first-time parents we were in no position to understand fully what it would mean—financially, emotionally, spiritually, and so on—to have a child. We didn't know if we were ready, or, if our reasons for delaying were insufficient, if we had to get ready, like it or not. There seemed to be no way to know; our conversations went in circles and never brought us closer to a firm decision.

In the end, we decided to pass the buck to God. Rather than trying to avoid conceiving or *really trying* to conceive, we just began playing a little bit fast and loose with the rules. Days that would have been off-limits just in case became fair game. It seems God was a bit more decisive than we were: Not long into the experiment, neither planned nor unplanned, Teresa Benedicta came into being.

Now, I'm not saying here that this is the only approach or even the best approach; it is, however, an approach that worked for us. After being very anxious to avoid conception for several months, I found this small act of submission to God's will to be incredibly freeing; there was no longer any pressure to play it safe, nor was there any new pressure *to conceive right now*. Relinquishing the dominion of my own decision-making does not come naturally to me, but the peace it brought was more than worth it.

And as far as little apocalypses go, Teresa has been quite a pleasant one.

Chapter 6

The Porn War

"We live in enemy-occupied territory."
— C. S. Lewis

By Dan S. Spencer III

I REMEMBER it like it was yesterday.

I had just finished giving a talk to a men's conference in the South. A middle-aged man approached me with tears in his eyes. He didn't have to say anything, but he did.

"My life is over. I've lost my job; my wife and kids have left me, I'm completely alone and not one of my friends has a clue of what I'm going through. Can you help me?"

It's the kind of question that takes your breath away and makes your pulse quicken. It's one thing to speak on the challenges of pornography and sexual integrity, but quite another to come face to face with a wounded, desperate man.

I noticed there were a couple dozen other men in line to say hello or comment on my talk. I asked if he could wait until I finished working the line so we could take some time to really discuss his situation. He agreed and so, after a few minutes, we met to discuss his issues. Sitting down in the first row of the church we began to work through his story, his shame, and his fears, and ultimately to explore a path forward.

I wish I could say he was the only desperate man I have met with over the past seven years. Unfortunately, every time I have spoken on radio or television, or at conferences or parishes, I have received similar requests and pleas for help.

If I am ever tempted to think the statistics citing pornography's size, scope, or devastation are exaggerated, those men remind me that, if anything, they are greatly *underestimated*. The sexual tsunami of pornography has touched tens of millions of men, their families, and communities. And it's getting worse.

Just a quick sample of the statistics and resulting issues of this spiritual war should be enough to give every man pause. Pornography:

- Porn revenue in the United States, all media: $13 billion[2]

- Percentage of men admitting workplace access to porn: 20%[3]

- Percentage of men who regularly visit porn websites: 72%[4]

- Percentage of adults admitting sexual addiction: 10%[5]

- 90% of children between ages 8 and 16 have seen pornography on the Internet[6]

- 47% of Christians say that pornography is a problem in the home[7]

- Adult film industry income: more than $4 billion per year—about the same as the NFL[8]

- Regular exposure to porn decreases sexual satisfaction in relationships for both men and women.[9]

NO SURPRISE

It is not a news alert that many men have struggled with or are struggling with sexual integrity. When I informally poll men about what percent of men they believe use pornography, the routine answer is "around twenty percent." This indicates just how uninformed most are about the scope and depth of this issue. One reason for this misjudgment is that pornography largely goes undiscussed and unreported. In many ways, it is similar to the manner in which abortion and its repercussions were ignored for decades.

Yet most of us, when the subject is brought up, respond as if this is something new. We respond as if we are sure *someone* is struggling with sexual issues, though certainly not *us*! And when we get even more specific and bring up the topic of the battle against pornography, the most common response I receive is: "Yeah, I've heard a little about that. Thank God I have never had to deal with that issue." Thank God indeed.

Even when Catholic leadership groups gather to discuss the challenges of sexual integrity and the need for leadership in this arena, men are reluctant to disclose their struggles. Very few are comfortable stepping up and admitting they are sexually compromised.

Nothing frightens most men more than having their mask removed.

REMOVING THE MASK

In a spiritual battle like this—a battle that affects so many men—we have little time to waste and even less time for pretending it doesn't exist. This is serious business, and men need to be educated and equipped to deal with it in their own life and in the lives of others.

Most men discuss a few basic subjects when we come together. We talk sports, business, the family, investments, politics, and so on. We engage in shallow discussions about these impersonal topics because as men we generally prefer to not discuss topics of a more *personal* nature in any depth. The majority of men simply refuse to disclose to another man any true vulnerability, pain, or problems. We just suck it up and get over it and keep it to ourselves.

Many men walk around with a "mask" so tightly attached that they begin to think it's their actual skin.

Men don't plan to fail. But frequently we do not have a real plan *to succeed*. And that is abundantly true in the area of our sexual integrity. The problem is that behind this sea of masks walking around in our businesses, schools, churches, and society, there are men grappling with some very tough realities, without any real knowledge, tools, or plan for resolving their difficulties.

STEPPING UP

Since most men simply don't want to open up about this issue, they need to begin thinking differently. In fact, to paraphrase Albert Einstein, we cannot solve our problems with the same thinking used when we created them. Men must begin with renewed thinking about pornography, understanding what it is, how it works, and why it's so devastating. That takes some courage, but wishing it all away is not going to get the job done. We need to step up.

THE BRAIN: THE LARGEST SEX ORGAN

One of the most fascinating developments in science over the past decade has been the explosion of new developments in brain science. How the brain works has never been more studied than it is today.

Men are hard-wired to respond physically to erotic images.[10] When men view porn, the brain releases a chemical called dopamine in unusually large amounts. This, in combination with testosterone, produces a heightened sense of excitement, causing the man to crave additional stimuli. Endorphins released into the brain further the extremely pleasurable sensations, and all of this, along with other naturally occurring hormones, triggers a desire for orgasm, which men act out through masturbation.[11]

The sad irony, of course, is that these chemicals and their responses were designed by God for an entirely different purpose. They are meant to be part of the natural organic rhythm of a married man with his wife. Physical attraction to her draws him to the natural and holy experience of sexual intercourse. Both spouses release a chemical called *oxytocin* before and during intercourse. This "bonding" hormone is designed to increase the sense of unity with one's spouse.[12]

Thus, God's creation is naturally experienced as a blessing within the context of lifelong, monogamous, marriage between one man and one woman. But in "solo-sex" there is no one to bond with, a situation that can lead to depression or deepen already existing depression.

Regardless of how or why men find themselves on this path, virtually all of them end up with a distorted and even violent vision of women and sexuality. The entire principle of love as total self-giving is turned upside down and becomes self-interested objectification. In focusing on himself, a man becomes ever more estranged from himself, God, and others. Professional counselors and therapists such as Dr. Patrick Carnes refer to the process of becoming ever more entangled in pornography as the "addictive cycle."[13]

In his book *Pure Desire*, former Marine fighter-pilot, recovered porn addict, and pastor Ted Roberts calls it *the noose*. In my experience with men, this is an appropriate term for the escalating process where we become just a shadow of what God intends us to be. Roberts likens the noose to a snare where the more the victim struggles to be released the tighter the noose becomes. And so it is when men, on their own, attempt to apply personal willpower to overcoming the attraction.[14]

THE "NOOSE"

So what is it, and how does it work?

Roberts reports that there are generally four components of this cycle:

1. The Causes

2. Resulting Mental Outlook

3. Ensuing Lifestyle

4. The Spiral Down

Causes

As anyone who has dealt with an inappropriate or addictive issue will attest, to conquer the problem you must understand and attack the root. There are underlying factors—root causes—almost always present in men struggling with pornography.

Primary causes include wounds received by being raised in a dysfunctional family, experiencing personal trauma at a young age, and being marinated in a "pornified" culture. For married men, marital conflicts and a failure to understand wholesome sexuality are common underlying issues.

Eventually, when a boy or man becomes more emotionally conflicted within himself about sexuality, he can slip into a mindset that leads to problems with porn.

The Mental Outlook

At this stage a man often has the sense that he is, in reality, not worthy of real love. Increasingly, he feels that not only is he worthless, but also that no one, if they truly knew him, would like him. He begins to feel desperate to avoid this pain and compensates with destructive coping behaviors that give an instant, if false, sense of joy and peace.

The Lifestyle

As this fantasy mentality takes hold of a man's brain, he becomes increasingly dependent on the experience and the attendant feelings. What began as viewing a basic image of nudity quickly escalates into a frantic need for increased stimulation. Simple "sin management" or "just say no" is rarely effective at this stage. He requires both human and divine assistance, but the shame and guilt he feels hold him captive.

The Spiral Down

As a result of this repeated fantasy, ritual acting out, and resulting secrecy, shame, and guilt, a man moves into a critical time in his downward spiral. For most, this is a time of vehement denial, but it is frequently at this point that many men begin to desire getting caught. They actually long to be released from the prison of sexual bondage.

Facing this fork in the road, a man will either go on denying and deluding himself or, by grace, become so desperate that he is willing to change. It is axiomatic that until someone seriously struggling with, or addicted to, pornography reaches this place of total surrender, he cannot truly heal. But if he does, he can be set free. And this is when God can work miracles.

Help & Hope

The good news is that there is help and hope for men struggling with pornography. Not all men are "addicted" to pornography. A great many are, however, at least afflicted by it. And while it would be impossible to describe all of the different approaches to helping men with this issue, there are some basics appropriate for all.

Jesus Is Our Source of Healing

Jesus came for wounded men. He loves the wounded, the bound, the afflicted, and the sick. He famously corrected those opposed to His reaching out to the wounded when He said, "It is not those who are healthy that need a physician, but those who are sick" (Mt 9:12, NASB). That reality is attested to repeatedly in Scripture in both action and parable. Jesus Christ wants men to be fully alive and to be set free from bondage. The road to recovery and freedom begins with our being "all in" with the great and ultimate Healer. Without this, the man of God will never be truly or completely free.

Wake Up

If men are ever going to successfully fight the porn wars, they need to get educated. Information by itself is not the answer, but remaining uninformed about the facts only increases the chances of falling into the problem. Every man needs a plan, based on facts, to "suit up" for life in our pornified culture.

Part of this reality is that men need to begin believing what the Scripture teaches about spiritual warfare and Satan. St. Peter himself told us to wake up: "Be sober [alert], be watchful. Your adversary the devil prowls around like a roaring lion, seeking some one to devour" (1 Pt 5:8, RSVCE).

Do you know which prey the lion attacks? Prey that has been wounded; prey that is weak; and prey that has wandered off alone from the herd.

FRIENDSHIP

Friends are critical to every aspect of the spiritual life. Rod Handley of the Character that Counts ministry says of male friendship:

1. Friends are not optional; they are essential.

2. Friends must be cultivated; they are not automatic.

3. Friends impact our lives; they are not neutral.[15]

Most men have many kinds of friends, but the majority are social or professional acquaintances. What a man truly needs is a friend who shoots straight with him, corrects him, encourages him, and prays for him. And when a man finds (and becomes) such a friend it allows him to take the next important step—speaking honestly about what's going on in his life.

The most significant reason men keep struggles to themselves is that the majority of men do not have even *ONE true friend* they can be completely honest, open, and transparent with. Recent social research indicates that all adults have approximately one-third fewer real friends in 2010 than in 1985. In the 2010 study, 48% claimed to have just one true friend, 18% claimed two, and 29% claimed more than two.[16] Four percent listed zero—a threefold increase from 25 years ago.

True masculine friendship is increasingly rare, with research showing that men begin to lose interest in close friends when they enter high school. They begin what are called "shoulder-to-shoulder" friendships and avoid face-to-face conversations, which they perceive as feminine.[17]

One result of this interpersonal alienation is that when troubling things do happen to men in the normal course of life, they simply ignore them or deal with them in an unhealthy manner. Hence men move to choices that are ultimately destructive for themselves and those around them.

ACCOUNTABILITY

Most men don't understand accountability. They frequently mistake it for responsibility. Rather, it is the willingness to share the reality of one's choices and resulting outcomes with another person in complete safety, honesty, and candor. It is also intended to be a two-way street. Helping others be accountable helps each partner in the conversation. Such a relationship, when shared with a true friend, can be amazingly liberating. Through accountability struggles become shared battles, and no man can fight, and win, this battle for purity and sexual integrity alone.

In the area of pornography it is wise to engage not only a companion on the quest for chastity, but also to employ technological tools. Software that reports to an accountability partner a history of your online Web visits is a powerful tool in fighting temptation. Tools such as those offered by Covenant Eyes are excellent for this purpose.

Our ultimate accountability experience is found in the Sacrament of Reconciliation. It is there that a man not only owns up to his own failures and is offered mercy regardless of his sin, but also, with proper contrition and commitment to amend his life, receives forgiveness and the sanctifying grace to continue fighting the evil one. This grace is part of the supernatural arsenal God gives us to fight evil by putting on "the whole armor of God, that you may be able to stand against the wiles of the devil" (Eph 6:11, RSVCE).

SPIRITUAL READING

Men, to their peril, frequently neglect spiritual reading. The Scriptures are the written word of God and are critical if men are to conform their minds to the mind of Christ (see Rom 12:2). Other spiritual reading can also build men up in Christ. Books and other writing by and about the saints are especially beneficial in this regard.

Further, recent popes and other Church leaders have given special attention to the issues men face and to sexual integrity and the fight against pornography specifically. Pope St. John Paul II gave us a treasure in the Theology of the Body, a series of teachings that can help us arrive at a much deeper and more holistic understanding of our sexuality. It is required reading for all of us who are serious about embracing the beauty of sexuality as we seek to renew our minds.[18]

Counseling

Most men, of course, fight the idea of going to a counselor, but counseling is a wonderful gift to the Church in the battle against pornography. Do you need a counselor? To arrive at an answer you must be honest with yourself.

In the first place, you need to determine if you are simply struggling with an unhealthy interest in pornography or if you are truly addicted. Many men go on binges of porn viewing followed by willful attempts to go cold turkey. This has limited value, and when they return to their habit they experience terrible frustration.

Some guidelines can help you understand the level of your problem. In his book *The Pornography Epidemic*, Peter Kleponis provides a self-assessment tool to help you determine where you are on the continuum.[19] If you're simply struggling with the recurring sin of viewing pornography, this can usually be addressed with some personal and technical accountability, reconciliation, support groups, and so on. If, however, you find yourself in the nearly daily bondage of viewing pornography, then you are best served by contacting a certified therapist to help you break free. A therapist is particularly skilled at uncovering wounds that are difficult to identify and articulate, traumatic events, and other issues that contribute to addiction. I highly recommend that you try to find a Catholic therapist, or at least one who supports the Catholic faith's approach to such treatment.

GROUP SUPPORT

The *My House* Catholic 12-step program—created by the Archdiocese of Kansas City in Kansas—is one model of a group support program, but there are many others such as Sexaholics Anonymous and similar efforts. These groups bring together people who struggle and who are looking for mutual support and a structured approach to overcoming their challenges. Groups are particularly helpful for introducing men to accountability partners. Wives of addicted men also often need additional and ongoing support and an extended period (six to twelve months) of individual counseling.

THE SACRAMENTS

Frequent reconciliation, as noted, is essential in a man's quest for purity, with this provision: a man should go to the same confessor regularly, not "shopping" priests to avoid the challenges of blunt, direct confessions. Most Catholic accountability groups require weekly use of reconciliation.

The Mass is the supreme opportunity to receive the graces necessary to continue the journey to chastity. Following a thorough confession men can humbly, but confidently, approach the altar to receive the body, blood, soul, and divinity of the Lord Jesus Christ—the ultimate healer of our body and soul. The sanctifying grace received in these sacraments is the greatest aid, empowering men with the gifts of mercy and strength to overcome temptation.

Prayer and Fasting

Many men think that fasting is a medieval practice to be pursued only during Lent. Still others think of it as a way to manipulate God into giving us what we want. Both understandings of this spiritual discipline are incorrect.

The Church didn't create fasting as a sort of punishment. Nor is it a practice only undertaken by cloistered religious as part of their order's charism. Rather, the Church recommends this practice for all Christians because Our Lord told us to do so as part of *normal Christian discipline*. That word—discipline—indicates why fasting can seem so difficult for a man who is struggling with sexual sin like pornography. For such a man, discipline is one of his obvious challenges in general, making *spiritual* discipline seem even more onerous.

Prayer can be a help in this regard, which is one reason why prayer and fasting always go together. One is an external expression while the other an internal expression, but both help us humble ourselves and focus on the issue at hand as we replace our desire with an intentional time of denial and prayer. Nothing focuses us more than abstaining from a normal habit—or engaging in an action outside our normal habits—for some particular purpose. Other reasons to pursue prayer and fasting include:

1. Scripture instructs us to do so.

2. The lives of the saints attest to the benefits of these practices.

3. The discipline involved helps us to build discipline into our lives, a benefit as we fight all sin and vice.

4. Prayer and fasting build humility. We come to acknowledge that the flesh is weak and in this place of renewed dependence on Christ we see that He is our strength and we can't rely on our own efforts.

5. Prayer and fasting give us hope that with Christ we can gain mastery of evils that attack the flesh.

6. These practices allow us to focus on particular struggles and virtuous solutions.

Self-Examination

Every man struggling with the challenges of pornography needs to create a practical plan to get on the path to sexual integrity and stay on it. When we think of self-examination we rightly think of the interior life, but we might also examine ourselves by thinking about the environment around us. Start by taking a good honest look around the house. Over time we become almost blind to items and conditions within our homes that might be stumbling blocks to sexual integrity and need serious attention. I call this "cleansing the temple." Just as Jesus took a whip to the unacceptable practices occurring in His Father's house, we need to take similar serious action against those items and practices in our homes that facilitate sexual sin.

Get rid of absolutely *everything* that tempts you to commit sexual sin! And don't kid yourself, this can be tough. Items like premium cable channels along with any media such as sports magazines, men's magazines, as well as suggestive college mementos, posters, music, videos, and so forth: it all has to go. Next, consider habits that put you in potentially dangerous situations such as going to bars, clubs, boys' night out events, even swimming pools if they are a temptation or near occasion of sin, as the Church calls them. Obviously, you need to also get rid of *any and all* pornographic materials. Finally, end any relationships with friends or acquaintances who do not embrace sexual integrity. This is all part of your new sobriety. Yes, this is tough, but if the effort seems especially difficult, perhaps that is an indication of the hold these things and people have on your life.

In addition to the above, here are some of the questions that can help identify other plan components:

1. Are there repetitive situations that lead me to think about porn?

2. Where do I usually access or think about pornography most often?

3. What time of day do I usually think about or access porn? Is there a pattern?

4. What "rituals" do I engage in immediately prior to acting out?

5. Are there any terms, words, or images that trigger unholy thinking?

6. Do I have friends who undermine my efforts or do not share my beliefs in purity?[20]

Men can and do beat the challenges they face in dealing with pornography. Consider your true identity in Christ and to make a commitment to be that man. As in most of the spiritual life, courage and tenacity are key. Contend for this holy goal of sexual integrity for yourself, your spouse and family, and, indeed, the whole of society. As St. John Paul II said so often, *Be not afraid!*

Recommended Resources

Counseling

Integrity Restored: www.IntegrityRestored.com

Accountability Software: Covenant Eyes: www.covenanteyes .com

General Information

The Porn Effect: www.theporneffect.com

Filter Review: www.filterreview.com

Family Safe Media: www.familysafemedia.com

Fathers for Good: www.fathersforgood.com

The Chastity Project: www.chastityproject.com

Diocesan Materials

My House: www.archkck.org/MyHouse

Help for Men

National Fellowship of Catholic Men: www.nfcm.net

St. Joseph Covenant Keepers: www.dads.org

Family Life Center: www.familylifecenter.net

Porn No More: www.pornnomore.com

Sexaholics Anonymous: www.sa.org

Books

Be a Man, by Father Larry Richards

Breaking Free: 12 Steps to Sexual Purity, by Steve Wood

Theology of the Body Made Simple, by Father Anthony Percy

Every Man's Battle, by Steve Arterburn

* * *

DAN SPENCER is a frequent national speaker, writer, and outspoken advocate for sexual integrity. He consulted on the Kansas City in Kansas, and Columbus, Ohio, diocesan anti-porn initiatives; is a board member of Men of Valor, the nation's largest sexual integrity conference for men; and is the Executive Director of the National Fellowship of Catholic Men. Besides privately coaching men struggling with pornography issues, his Accountability Outline is used by dozens of Catholic men's groups around the nation every week. Dan and Linda, his wife of 39 years, live in Overland Park, Kansas, near their four married children and seven grandchildren.

CHAPTER 7

Re-learning Gratitude:
The Vocation of an Infertile Father

By Timothy P. O'Malley, Ph.D.

I OFTEN wonder what goes through the mind of my son on those occasions when he smiles so intensely that it looks like his face has been occupied by joy itself. Indeed, there are moments in my life when I, too, have shared in such superabundant joy. The first day as an undergraduate at the University of Notre Dame, I found myself supremely blissful to be walking in the presence of the glistening Golden Dome. My wedding day was another such occasion, in which the sheer gift of the moment occupied my attention from the dawning of light on that December winter day to the glistening darkness of an Indiana landscape blanketed with layers of fresh snow. The day that I defended my doctoral dissertation, the moment that Notre Dame defeated the University of Southern California in November 2010, watching in person the Boston Celtics play in the NBA Finals—at these moments, I have known the possibility of joy.

But my toddler son's experience of joy is entirely different than my own. For him, the gift of joy is a constant possibility. The stacking of bowls within the confines of our kitchen brings forth both attention and laughter beyond what mere mortals thought possible. The opening and closing of our front door elicits a delight that is unspeakable by the limited instrument of the human tongue. My arrival at home after a long day of grading, teaching, and sending soul-deadening e-mails is marked by my son's speedy crawl toward me, then arms raised in wonder at what he perceives at my sudden and unexpected presence in his midst. Thomas Joseph is capable of perceiving all of creation as pure gift.

The reader may, of course, note that the arrival of my son was not listed among those moments of joy catalogued above. The absence of this moment is more than a gaffe by a father and husband whose greatest moments of joy (and crushing sadness) have occurred while watching the University of Notre Dame's football team on Saturdays in autumn. Rather, the advent of my son is an event that is categorically different than any moment of my life thus far. For, as a member of an infertile couple, I had ceased expecting to find myself gazing into the eyes of a child who would call me "Dad." Yet, in a flash, on that late December afternoon in a city away from our home of South Bend, Indiana, I found myself face-to-face with my newly adopted son who would not only learn to call me "Dad," but would also express this relationship through gifting me with sleepless nights, exploding diapers, and a renewed vision of every day, of every moment, as sheer, exhilarating gift.

Thus the narrative I hope to catalog in these pages is not one in which I am appealing to the pathos of readers who have come to perceive the suffering plight of an infertile couple. Rather, I hope to offer an account of a life in which infertility and then adoption have slowly reformed me in the practice of gratitude. Through taking up infertility as a Eucharistic vocation, I have learned to once again gaze upon every fiber of creation as a gift to be received and then offered back to the God who is total gift.

THE VOCATION OF INFERTILITY

As a theologian concerned with the formation of Christian identity, I often find myself involved in lengthy discussions about vocation with undergraduates. Among deeply committed Catholic undergraduates at Notre Dame, the language of vocation permeates life around campus. Undergraduate women and men assemble to discuss a desire for consecrated life or the priesthood. Likewise, marriage occupies the attention of many of my students, who wonder if they are called to the sacrament of marriage with *this* boyfriend or girlfriend. Students seek to discern whether or not they are called to *this* major, *this* career, *this* internship, or *this* summer service project. In each instance, the students hope to establish a series of criteria through which they might discern whether they are acting according to God's plan for their lives.

These students tend to think of vocation as fulfilling their desires and needs, but they can't imagine the cost that often comes with a life that has been submitted to God's loving hands. The dreams we have about our future—what we imagine our vocation to be—will eventually have to come to terms with a world in which all possibilities are not possible. The key to vocation is not learning to find your career or to discern your future partner or religious order, but learning to enter entirely into the mysterious will of the triune God.

The problem with teaching or parenting is that you often find yourself having to listen to your own advice. For years, I led students into a richer conception of what constitutes Christian vocation relative to this "letting go" into the divine will. I stated with the sort of certitude reserved for the inexperienced that nothing that happens within our lives is outside of God's gift of Providence. Even in the darkest moments, the possibility of divine love is still present, calling us to perceive anew the wondrous love of the God who became flesh.

When we encounter this darkness within the contours of our lives, we are not to turn away from it. Instead, we are to enter more deeply into the darkness, aware that only through the giving away of ourselves can we learn to see the presence of the crucified and risen Christ dwelling in the depths of our lonely sorrow.

Of course, when my wife and I learned that we were un-explainably infertile, I never thought about what I had been teaching to young adults for the previous seven years. I had imagined my vocation as husband unfolding as a natural move-ment from epic wedding, to successful career, to the presence of precocious children, and eventually to a comfortable home in some sleepy college town where we would raise our brood of five or so to read Augustine in the presence of a small, albeit deeply interesting and slightly nerdy, community of friends. Faced with the reality of infertility, I saw that this "dream" would be nothing more than that.

Yes, there were medical options that were offered to us, in-cluding in vitro fertilization (we were told that we were ideal candidates for this procedure). Such an option was ultimately not one that we even considered as faithful Catholics. We knew that this procedure, however much it might soothe our own sorrow, would necessarily involve the creation of embryos that would never survive. While we often wished that the Church's pastoral care toward infertile couples would be more robust, we could not sacrifice a single life so that we might experience the gift of a child.

In the midst of this disorienting departure from my nar-rative of happiness, I certainly never questioned the gift of my marriage. Kara and I maintained a deep and abiding love for one another. Yet every other aspect of my vocation came under question in the days following our awakening to what it might mean to be infertile. I wondered about the validity of worship-ing and studying a God who allowed such pain to happen to couples such as us. I could not attend Mass without a deep sense of envy toward those friends who seemed to reproduce almost by accident.

My life of intimate communion with God grew fallow as I slowly tired of uttering prayers for children to a God whose lack of interest in my life seemed to grow more obvious by the day. My love of Kara never ceased. But I no longer lived the vocation of marriage as a form of life dedicated to a transformation of the cosmos through sharing Christ's own love with world. I had grown to hate God and the world alike.

I remember the day at Mass in our parish in South Bend where I finally recognized that I had been treating infertility less as an occasion to grow into the prodigal gift of Christ's love and more as an idol of sorrow. Sitting to my left were our dearest friends, who at the time were pregnant with their third child. For months, I had been avoiding spending time with the whole family, aware that every encounter with them was both a reminder of my barrenness and an invitation to revisit questions about the existence of God that had been nagging me during the infertile years.

My attention turned to the crucifix at the front of my otherwise artistically beige parish, and for the first time in several years, I actually prayed the Eucharistic Prayer. Slowly, I became aware that each of us in the assembly that day were offering the entirety of our lives to the Father through the Son, who knows the fullness of what it means to be human. My sorrow, however real, was not the only pain present in that assembly. To my right was the elderly parishioner who attends the bedside of his wife after each Eucharistic liturgy, aware that this visit might be his last. In front of me stood a recently homeless man who knows what it is like to be treated as less than human by those who pass him by. Families throughout that parish, even ones that live seemingly without any visible imperfection, endure the pain of affairs that rip apart husband and wife, of children who suffer from depression, of the disappointing awareness that domestic life is not quite what they had hoped for it to be.

In *this* parish, in *this* moment, Christ was offering the entirety of humanity's pain and sorrows to the Father in love. And through the Spirit, Christ was inviting us to see anew how total, self-giving love, even in the midst of these sorrows, could transfigure creation. For the first time, I came to see the intellectual possibility that infertility might not be an expression of divine silence but instead could function as an invitation to a more radical form of God-shaped love. Infertility might be the way that God was speaking to us.

Several weeks after this moment, my wife Kara suggested that we attend an upcoming training for foster-care parents. I recoiled from the suggestion immediately. To become a foster parent would be akin to a final rejection of my dream of a perfect family and of a sophisticated community of learners in that sleepy college town. Foster parenting is temporary. It is not about having children come to visit you at the holidays when you are retired, but caring for children for a period of time until they can be re-integrated into their biological families. That's not what I wanted. I wanted children *who were mine!* Yet, as we sat in that even more beige government building and were presented with the needs of these children, I finally came to see my infertility as vocation. I came to recognize that I was called to have a family, but one not defined by the rather limited vision of happiness that I had been operating out of.

Kara and I have been called to infertility; it is our vocation, so that our love might move beyond biological bounds to all those who need to know the gift of Eucharistic love in their lives. We are called to foster, to adopt, to allow our darkness to become a visible sign of divine love for the world. Now, we recognize that this is not an automatic decision for infertile couples. Adoption is not a requirement or possibility for many infertile couples, who may make a prudent decision based upon household economics or emotional state not to adopt.

Nor for that matter does adoption make the pain of infertility disappear. While your friends have a second or third child, you'll still be infertile. Instead, both foster care and adoption alike were ways that we, only after a process of discernment, could offer our infertility on the Eucharistic altar of the Church, allowing it to become transformed into a gift for the life of the world.

Infertility, for us, is no longer a curse. It is not the deepest pain of our lives. Rather, it has become a gift that opens us to love all those who know the depths of sorrow. My vocation to fatherhood was not eliminated because we were unable to have children. Instead, my vocation to fatherhood has taken a shape different from the one that I supposed, from the one that I had hoped for. I had to let go of the vision of happiness that I had constructed on my own and receive anew the Eucharistic vision of sacrificial love that Christ revealed. I had to see infertility as a vocation, a gift.

THE GIFT OF ADOPTION

Of course, infertility is *now* only part of our story. In the year before we were certified as foster parents, Kara and I had also been approved by a local adoption agency. The hope for a child that dawned with the conclusion of the approval process had slowly been overshadowed by the anxious longing and then self-protective forgetfulness ("Oh yeah, we're on a list to adopt.") characteristic of infertile, adoptive parents.

In the fall of 2012, we found ourselves very close to a number of foster placements with no contact from our adoption agency. In early December 2012, this changed. Kara received a phone call from our social worker, letting her know that we had been chosen by a birth mother. In the midst of final exams, a wedding in Ireland, and a Christmas planned in Tennessee, we prepared during the season of Advent for the arrival not simply of the Christ Child but of a newborn son of our own.

In the octave of Christmas, we found ourselves driving south to the hospital where our son was to be born. The plan for the day involved us arriving at the hospital, waiting for the birth of our son, and then spending forty-eight hours in the hospital until we could adopt. Beforehand, we had been told that the birth mother would not want to see us. Yet when we arrived at the hospital, we learned that she had changed her mind and wanted to see us right before Tommy was born.

What would we say? "Thank you for this incredible gift" didn't quite seem adequate for the occasion. How can you adequately thank another human being for the gift of a person? Perhaps it would be more appropriate to offer a vision of the life that we hoped to give to her son? Yet that seemed to turn the whole moment into a kind of exchange, where we received another person's son because of the life that we could offer him. Soon the moment arrived for us to meet the birth mother of our son, and before we could proffer a note of gratitude, she thanked us.

As an infertile couple we had never considered the possibility that we would receive thanks for adopting Thomas. The gift of Thomas Joseph into our lives was gift beyond gift, an event in which no act of gratitude could function as a return gift for what we received. Yet the birth mother viewed our action as gift. This moment of mutual gratitude, however small it may appear to an observer, has colored every moment of being a father since Thomas Joseph has arrived in my life.

At a fundamental level, the arrival of my son has permanently altered the way that I view infertility. Whereas before Thomas's quite sudden entrance into our home, I slowly began to see infertility as a vocation, a gift, I now can perceive in the concrete presence of my son the fruits of the gift of infertility. The presence of this particular person in my life, a person in whose conception I had no responsibility, has himself become gift beyond gift. I delight in his being, constantly surprised by his presence in my life. He is not mine in a biological sense of the term, yet he is profoundly mine in the order of love.

In the year and a half since he entered our lives, I now find it a virtual impossibility to imagine *not being infertile*. For without our infertility, without the very real pain of not being able to have a child, I never would have received the gift of this particular smile, this particular toddler tackle, this particular person in my life. I know that Thomas Joseph will not be a toddler forever. I know that like all children he will one day make a concerted effort to avoid hugs, kisses, and general time spent in the presence of his father. Yet every one of these moments, just like every late-night diaper change or feeding, exists in the order of gift.

I have also learned to see that adoption reveals a general truth about fatherhood. The reality is that most parents come to see their children as an extension of our own identities. We may begin to imagine that this child really is exactly like us, thinking like us, behaving like us, becoming us. Yet every child (biological or adopted) is never really ours to begin with. We receive the gift of a child in our lives only to watch this toddler begin to develop a conscious identity that is apart from us. My son refuses to eat as an act of rebellion; he ignores us when we tell him not to do something; and he throws tantrums when we stop him from doing something that might kill him.

The reality is that every child is a unique, historical person who is not reducible to either the genetic material of parents or the social world made possible by life in this family. And the presence of this child in our lives, the love of this child for us, comes itself as a gift that we could never have imagined. Fatherhood is not about trying to replicate one's own identity in another creature. Instead, authentic fatherhood strives to form the child in the reality of gift at the heart of creation. Biological or adopting dads are most fully fathers when they form the imaginations of their children in the practice of gratitude.

The gift of adoption is that I now know the nature of gratitude. The gift of our infertility is that I now know what it means to enter into the mysterious will of God, to let go of every notion of happiness that I thought essential, and still see the presence of divine love on the other side. When we tell our son that he is adopted, these are the gifts I seek to give. I want him to know that he is loved by so many people, including his birth mother. I want him to know how much we love him. But, I want him to know most of all that his adoption, if he has the eyes to see, was the result of total and absolute gift. Not merely the gift of his biological mother. Not merely the gift of his adopting parents. But the gift of a God who has formed the world as oriented toward love itself.

POSTURE OF GRATITUDE

Adopting Thomas Joseph because of our infertility has reawakened me to the sheer wonder of the gift that we receive as those who live under the protection of divine love. What I had never imagined possible, having a son of my own, has become the organizing principle in my life. He follows me around the house, and I enter into his own imaginative world where stacked-up bowls, slammed doors, and giant stuffed caterpillars are occasions that elicit joyful wonder. He has invited me to see reality for what it is, pure and total gift. And my own vocation as adopting father will be to invite him to return this gift of love in the Eucharistic life of the Church.

Because of this primordial gift at the heart of creation, the gift that we call God, I constantly remember that Thomas' love for me (and my love for Tommy) is not the fullness of the happiness I am called toward. Tommy and I are called to a deeper gratitude than either of us is capable of giving on our own. He will one day cease giving me the fullness of his attention, and, at times, will undoubtedly express a lack of gratitude for the love that his mother and father have offered him. I, even now, forget to see in him an occasion for total gratitude in the midst of the busyness of my schedule.

Yet there is good news. We are called to enter into the reality of love, of self-gift, that is God. All of us have been adopted not merely into some family in South Bend. Our adoption has been into the baptismal and Eucharistic love of the triune God, who seeks to awaken us more and more each day to the gift of life itself. For one, I am grateful that my vocation to infertile fatherhood serves as a constant sign of this reality. Through infertility, I have learned what it means to be a baptized Catholic, one who is learning to practice a posture of gratitude even in the midst of the toils and tribulations that mark our lives. For even in our greatest sorrow, God's love can transform the darkness into light.

* * *

TIMOTHY P. O'MALLEY, Ph.D., is director of the Notre Dame Center for Liturgy and teaches in the Department of Theology, University of Notre Dame. He is the author of *Liturgy and the New Evangelization: Practicing the Art of Self-Giving Love* (Liturgical Press, 2014). He and his wife, Kara, live in South Bend, Indiana, and have one son.

CHAPTER 8

Raising Our Children in the Faith:
A Grateful Convert

By Kevin Lowry

I'M a convert to fatherhood.

As a young man in our hedonistic culture, my pursuits were decidedly self-centered. Yet God had other plans. The ball began rolling toward fatherhood when, as a Presbyterian (and son of a Presbyterian minister, no less), I attended a small Catholic college called Franciscan University of Steubenville. The first time, due to my enthusiastic pursuit of the social activities of the school, I got kicked out.

After being somewhat miraculously readmitted three years later, I met an incredible, beautiful young woman. She was Wesleyan. We took an "ethics" course together, studying the

1968 encyclical *Humanae Vitae*, which reaffirmed the Catholic Church's historic teaching about artificial contraception. Wow. I had never heard the Church's teachings on the subject of artificial birth control—a nonissue for Presbyterians—but it turned into the tipping point for my appreciation of Catholicism. I found myself hurtling inexorably toward the Church, beautiful young woman in tow.

Not long after taking that ethics course, my conversion to fatherhood, and Catholicism, was complete. The beautiful young woman and I got married and had our first three kids in less than three years (no twins, just awesome chemistry). Together, we became Catholic. We went on to have five more kids. Two of our kids have now had weddings of their own. We just had our first grandchild, and now understand that children are just a means to having grandchildren.

As it stands right now, we have eight children, ages seven to twenty-four, two daughters-in-law, and—did I mention?—a grandchild. We're beyond excited about that. Only the four youngest kids still live at home, including one who is medically fragile. As I write this, he's recovering from an emergency surgery at Children's Hospital in Columbus, Ohio. I'm grateful to be a father, but it isn't always easy.

Sweet Humiliation

Somehow through the journey of parenthood that began over two decades ago, my wife and I went from being energetically idealistic to wearily pragmatic. There's only one thing that has been absolutely abiding, unshakable, constant, written in stone.

I love my kids.

In a spirit of full disclosure, my kids are very much works in process, as am I, and as are we all. We've encountered many struggles along the path, including some tumultuous teenage years. I'm not going to list all the challenges my kids have faced (that's really their story to tell), but they've been many and varied. Can issues such as unchastity impact faithful Catholic families? Sadly, the answer is yes. There have been other issues too, probably some I don't even know about. When you're a parent, at times your intel is less than perfect, which causes further difficulties. It's hard to prescribe a remedy when you're unsure of the diagnosis.

In the worst of times, I have been overwhelmed, looking deep within myself for the sources of our children's struggles. We did everything we knew to give them a good upbringing: they were part of an intact family; their mom stayed home; they were home-schooled; they got involved in parish and extracurricular activities; they were faithfully taken to Mass, steeped in the sacraments, prayed with, encouraged, and *loved*.

We had this perfect plan, but the reality didn't even come close. So what happened? For years, that question has bounced around my mind as I tried to figure out where I went wrong. I worked too much. I didn't spend enough quality time with them. I provided a poor example. I endowed them with faulty genes. What happened to that idealistic twenty-something father who dared to be critical of parents whose teens went off the rails?

A BAD PARENTING MOMENT

The truth is I haven't always been a faithful example. One particular instance, probably among my worst ever parenting moments, remains vivid in my mind.

Several years ago, two of my teenage boys shared a room. One night I had asked the boys to be quiet and to go to sleep several times, becoming increasingly frustrated as I stressed out over trying to get enough sleep to be semi-lucid for a big meeting at work the next day. Sometime around midnight I was completely beyond my coping mechanisms. I heard laughter emanating from the boys' room—again—and snapped.

With a forced calmness, I walked into their room. They looked at me and, once again, *broke out laughing*. It would be difficult to describe the flood of emotions I experienced in that moment. In addition to being exhausted, grouchy, fed up, and stressed out, I now felt completely disrespected. "Come with me," I said.

Leading them downstairs, I opened the front door and motioned toward the snow-covered front yard. In a calm voice, I said, "Get the *$&#! out of my house."

Wide-eyed, they shuffled past me in their shorts and T-shirts into the bitter winter cold. I locked the door and went back to bed.

I let them back in a few minutes later. Yes, my wife's shocked reaction had something to do with that. The boys apologized, especially about laughing when I came into the room; they said it wasn't at me, but was in the context of what they had been talking about right before I entered. I apologized, too. Everyone survived.

At the same time, this is precisely the kind of thing I wish I had done differently. Were there an infinite number of better ways to handle the situation? You better believe it.

I was humbled through this experience. Humiliated, in fact. With the benefit of hindsight, however, I wonder whether that was exactly what I needed.

Joy in Tribulations

You see, I may be older and less energetic, and I may have made many more mistakes than twenty years ago, but my love for my kids has grown. Flourished. Deepened. Hardened. No matter what they do. It's because of who they are.

In fact, one of the things I used to tell them is: "I don't care so much about *what you do* when you grow up, I care about *who you are*." As it turns out, the sanctification that I desire so deeply for them continues. Not quite so expectedly, so does my own.

One of my favorite parables in the Bible is the story of the prodigal son. What I've begun to appreciate in time is that identifying the story just as "the prodigal son" is profoundly incomplete. Yes, it's about the son—both sons, in fact. But even more so, it's about the father.

When the story begins, the son is in the process of dishonoring his father in the most selfish, disrespectful way possible. By claiming his half of the inheritance, the son was, in effect, saying that he wished his father were dead. Even through this, the father loved the son. He honored his selfish wishes, gave him the money, and allowed him to go.

Then he waited. And he hoped. And he prayed.

When the son finally reappeared, the father ran to meet him, embraced him, and gave him a place of honor. The father wasn't concerned about himself. He had been humbled. Humiliated, in fact. It was probably through this experience that he became a great father.

The father's trials caused his love to increase.

GOD THE FATHER

One day when I was particularly despondent over the plight of one of my older children, a faithful friend attempted to cheer me up: "You can't judge yourself by your children's decisions. Remember that God was the father to Adam and Eve."

It hit me like a bolt of lightning. In my pride, I had been holding myself to a higher standard than God himself. My friend was right.

God created free will. Now, free will is a double-edged sword. Without it, love isn't possible. At the same time, free will makes us capable of sin. Yet there is something remarkably beautiful about the Christian life: God uses even our mistakes to build us up. This is true both for parents and for our children.

I've been built up a ton over the last twenty-five-plus years. Fatherhood, in fact, has served to enrich my life in ways I wouldn't trade for *anything*. I love my kids, I adore my wife more than ever, and I love our lives together. Each of my children—without exception, asterisk, or small-print disclaimer—is a supreme gift.

The challenge is that even with a perfect example, as God certainly was in Eden, children have free will, too. My children have by God's grace witnessed much good parenting over the years, but they've also seen more than one bad parenting moment. Yet whether our example as parents is good, bad, or somewhere in between, our children respond differently. Even kids within the same family, with the same parents, can use their free will differently—and with diverse outcomes.

That certainly doesn't mean that our example doesn't matter. It does. But we need to be prepared to increasingly honor the free will of our children, even when they use it in ways we don't like. It's the same way God treats us.

Lessons Learned

Along the path of parenthood, there have been a remarkable number of lessons learned—and subsequently forgotten, so I've had to relearn them. However, there are a few themes that give me hope. By all means, avoid my manifold mistakes, but even with the mistakes, there are undeniable signs of hope.

Love Your Wife

Marriage is the underrated sacrament. So much good arises from a solid marriage, yet marriage is also hard to live out—and at best, we only control fifty percent of the equation.

It took me a few years of marriage to figure this out, but my wife needs regular, sustained attention and affection. So in time we got into a few habits that we both really enjoyed, like regular dates on Friday nights.

When the kids were young, it might only consist of bringing home take-out food and eating in another room—but we had that regular time focused on one another. We also had what we called "pillow parties," where the kids got to bring pillows and blankets to the family room and watch a DVD while mom and dad had time alone elsewhere in the house. They loved it, and we did, too.

It's impossible to overstate the importance of loving your wife, and similarly impossible to summarize how to do so in a couple of paragraphs. Just keep loving her, and recognize that this love (much like fatherhood) often takes the form of radical service, even if just in very small ways. Pray for her; never stop dating her; encourage her; learn more about her; listen to her; honor her; express affection to her; help her. Then do it again tomorrow.

The effect of all this is to model the type of self-giving that reminds us of our relationship with God. Loving our wives and honoring the sacrament of marriage is a foundational element in being a good example for our kids. A faithful, loving marriage carried out over the course of many years and through countless obstacles can only help lead our children to God. In addition, it helps to train our children so that someday they can have good marriages of their own.

Channel Your Dad Guilt

As a younger man, I worked like a maniac in my CPA firm and did my level best to provide for our rapidly expanding family. This meant late nights at the office, working on weekends, and often being distant—lost in my thoughts even when I was physically present. This torturous existence drove me crazy for many years.

I remember praying, going to confession frequently, meeting with a spiritual director, going on retreats, attending men's groups—you name it. Although all were invaluable, there was a never-ending tension between providing for the family financially and upholding my other responsibilities as a husband and father. It wasn't easy. Along the way, I changed jobs twice specifically to gain a better work/life balance.

Balance is always a struggle. If you do happen to get into a state of complete equilibrium, chances are it only lasts a moment. So I began to appreciate that the struggle is ongoing, difficult, and worthy. I learned to get better at some things, like working hard throughout the day, foregoing some social opportunities, and making appointments for my family, treating them like my most important client. Incrementally, these things all helped. But, finally, something happened that changed everything.

We had a special-needs son. What a blessing.

You see, all of a sudden my priorities changed. Like a light switch being flicked on, it was instantaneous. My wife was overwhelmed and needed help. It wasn't optional. My kids needed me in a whole new way. There were fears, tears, and prayers. Throughout the crisis surrounding our son's birth (which we were unsure he would survive), everything was put into its proper place.

I ended up leaving my CPA firm and placing a much higher premium on being able to spend time with my family. Perhaps it didn't result in maximum financial gain, but who cares? Friends of mine have Corvettes and Lexuses, but I have a Joseph. A David. A Hannah. And so on. They're gifts much more precious than money or things.

At one point later in my career, I left the corporate world entirely to join the staff of The Coming Home Network International, a small Catholic nonprofit apostolate. I took an enormous pay cut. However, it was completely worth it. I was able to spend more time with my family, and even more important, I was extremely happy to demonstrate—in concrete terms—that my role in the family involves more than maximizing our financial position. As my dad used to tell me, "Money is like air, you need a certain amount to live, but it's not the reason for living." Amen. Money is important, but it's not the most important thing in life.

This core belief explains why, when our medically challenged son winds up in Children's Hospital in Columbus, we're all reminded how much he matters—and how blessed we are to be a family. Dad guilt never did me much good, unless it led to positive changes. In this case, I took the week off and made a conscious decision not to stress out over work.

FAMILIES NEED PRAYER

This probably goes without saying, but there never seems to be a shortage of things to pray for in a family. Besides, prayer is the most fundamental aspect of our relationship with God. It's a beautiful thing to introduce children into a routine of regular, daily prayer.

As a family, it took us far too many years to figure this out. We knew other families who went to daily Mass, prayed a Rosary, memorized Bible verses, and worked at the soup kitchen, and whose kids were exegetical geniuses by age seven. That wasn't us.

We needed to figure out something that worked in our family life. Eventually we began saying a decade of the Rosary together each evening, and praying for one another and other intentions. Modest, you think? Yes, but it works for us. The important thing is to pray for the grace even to pray as a family and to do what works for you.

There will never be a substitute for prayer, and prayer of all kinds. Prayers of thanksgiving, prayers of intercession, prayers of devotion, prayers of worship, prayers for others, prayers for ourselves: these are all so important. If we can teach our children the importance of prayer by doing it more ourselves, and arranging life to include family prayer, how awesome is that?

Be a Good Example

A friend of mine used to joke that his best strategy for golf would be to take six months off and then quit. After some bouts with skin cancer, I decided to do just that. I wasn't much of a golfer anyway, and I couldn't justify the time away from the family. Some guys pull it off, but given my work schedule and other commitments at the time, it would have detracted too much from family life.

In so many ways, love involves self-sacrifice. This isn't even so much about the big things, but rather the little everyday things we do. Do we demonstrate a good work ethic? Tell people please and thank you? Say we're sorry when we've done something wrong? Are we gracious winners and losers? Do we model temperance by declining that third cookie after dinner? Are we generous toward others?

Personal sanctity is really an important element of parenthood, not to mention marriage. We must model docility to the Lord in order to set an example for our children to follow in later years. I remember vividly my father doing this for me. One early morning as a young adult, after being out partying all night, I recall coming in and seeing my dad praying. Despite being rather bleary-eyed at the time, even through my fog I recognized the stark juxtaposition.

It took quite a while for me to get on the right path, but eventually fatherhood itself served as part of the impetus. Being a dad naturally involves us getting out of ourselves and allowing our selfish motives to die slow deaths. Of course, there's an upside—we become better people. And I've never regretted putting greater emphasis on the family.

A case in point is father-son or father-daughter trips. I have been on several over the years, and they remain among my favorite memories. Along with a bunch of dads from an Opus Dei group in Pittsburgh, we visited the battlefields at Gettysburg a couple times, as well as a coal mine in eastern Pennsylvania.

The value of these types of activities is to connect us more closely with our children. There is an endless supply of rich historical treasures to explore, people and saints to learn from, and places to visit. It helps us all to feel a sense of belonging to the family—after all, getting to know our parents better helps us to understand ourselves.

Keep on Loving You

Like all members of the body of Christ, my children (and their parents) have sinned. At times, this has created an enormously heavy burden, and my prayers could hardly be more plaintive. The simple phrase "Lord Jesus Christ, have mercy on us" has emanated from my lips to God's ear countless times. Through the depths of our struggles, and despite gut-wrenchingly painful trials, I learned a simple lesson: I love my kids for who they are, not what they do. This is precisely how God regards us: He never gives up, no matter what. How comforting!

I have one son who has left the Church. This was a hard blow to my wife and me, and yet another trial that left us questioning our parenting acumen and example. Yet after absorbing the disappointment, we resolved simply to continue loving him. To this day my wife goes to Mass twice each week—once for her, once for him. We don't beat him over the head with a catechism every time we see him, but have redoubled our efforts to serve as models of unconditional love while not backing down from our beliefs.

While respecting the free will of God's creatures—our children—we are also tasked with forming their consciences, leading them to love God, family members, and others. So there's a balancing act. While the activities and behaviors of younger children are much easier to influence, the character formation process doesn't end when they turn eighteen. At that point, we have less influence than with a toddler, but it's still far north of zero.

So how do we handle this with older children? One way is to challenge their intellect and to question the underlying assumptions behind their beliefs and actions. Particularly when this is done from a standpoint of love, it can lead to fruitful discussions. And when combined with copious amounts of prayer, it can lead to changes of heart.

The one thing I remind our wayward adult child is this: he's only one confession away from being back in a complete state of grace. I pray for this *metanoia* (change of heart) for him, and take solace in the fact that God loves him even more than I do. As the saying goes, God has kids, but no grandkids.

Don't Stop Believing

In the end, there is tremendous value in the struggles of fatherhood. One of my favorite Scripture passages is found in the Letter to the Romans:

We rejoice in our sufferings, knowing that suffering produces endurance, and endurance produces character, and character produces hope, and hope does not disappoint us, because God's love has been poured into our hearts through the Holy Spirit who has been given to us. (5:3-5, RSVCE)

So the truly Christian response to trials and tribulations is, as always, to hope. I pray, my friend, that your path of parenthood will be less strenuous than mine. You will have every opportunity to be a much better example along the way, and you may well experience far better "outcomes" among your brood. But know that I wouldn't trade my journey for any other. Even our mistakes have left us stronger. Our scars endure, but God's grace has overcome even the most dire struggles and hardship.

In the end, we have hope. We know that conversion is a task beyond even the most capable parent. Our job is to plant seeds, to love, to encourage, to do everything possible to lead our children to Christ and His Church. Yet the conversion we covet—for our children and for ourselves—is ultimately the work of the Holy Spirit. We remain firmly ensconced in a place where we need mercy. All of us.

My son David should be able to leave the hospital soon. It has been a rough week and a half as he recovers from the emergency surgery. My wife hasn't left his side the entire time. I hope his future holds less time in hospitals, and more time pursuing his many creative interests. (He wants to be an inventor, and I think he'll be a good one.) But I still don't care as much what he does as who he is. Based on his many challenges in life, I'm confident God has plans for David, and the rest of us. There's always reason for hope. Besides, we're all just one confession away from a state of grace.

* * *

KEVIN LOWRY has spent more than twenty years in secular and nonprofit financial and executive roles. He is the author of *Faith at Work: Finding Purpose Beyond the Paycheck.* Kevin and his wife live in Columbus, Ohio, and have eight children.

CHAPTER 9

In the World, but Not of It: Deepening Our Children to Engage a Shallow Culture

By Tod Worner

THERE was little question in my mind. Everything had changed in an instant. *Absolutely everything.* On February 2, 2007, my first daughter, Annabel, came into the world. And she was *perfect.* With big blue eyes, a heart-melting toothless smile, and the sweetest handgrip barely able to encircle my thumb, I was utterly captivated. And then came another. On July 10, 2009, little Vivian joined us with a vivacious beauty and puckish charm of her own. Perfection had met her equal. The moment I laid eyes on these two gorgeous creatures— God's perfect creations—three things became very clear. First, my life would never be the same. Second, I couldn't love anything more deeply. And, finally, I would do anything for my two little girls.

The early years of child-rearing raced by in a blur. Late nights filled with inconsolable crying, voracious feedings, and concerning fevers gave way to teetering first steps, stubborn potty training, and water fights in the bathtub. Before long, the diaper bag was stowed, the booster replaced the car seat, and chess games or twenty questions were no longer easy to win. My daughters were growing up.

Looking at them both today with their smiling eyes, infectious giggle, and innocent wit, I couldn't be more proud. But pressing questions have started to crowd my mind. Is there some way to preserve their innocence? Is there a trick to ensure that a sweet joke always makes them laugh? Can I possibly prevent that wince of inevitable heartache from diminishing the light in their eyes? It's what every parent wants, but can't have. We want our kids' lives to be perfect and painless in an imperfect world.

My first daughter was born in the heart of an icy Minnesota winter. As my wife and daughter were discharged from the hospital, that child was the most well-bundled, securely seated, and cautiously driven newborn the world has ever known. We recognized the priceless life we had in our possession and would do anything to protect it. But just as dangerous drivers or unanticipated ice patches can lay waste to the best laid plans to protect our child's ride home, ill-blowing winds of culture risk adversely impacting our children as they grow older and begin to inch away from our protective embrace.

Our Catholic faith teaches us that God created the world. And He called it "good." God created man and woman. And He considered them dignified. By granting dignified humanity stewardship over a grand creation, we have been given an incredible opportunity to live fully and to achieve great things for the glory of God. And yet, man's original sin marred paradise and introduced imperfection.

And what are the results? The sweetest culture has become sour. The virtues of courage, temperance, prudence, and justice find themselves overshadowed by unapologetic decadence, mean-spirited selfishness, and an indifference to the truth. As a consequence, callousness, hopelessness, and cynicism become the prevailing ethos of the culture. What comes soon thereafter is nihilism, which is defined as a rejection of moral and religious principles, which can lead to the darkness of meaninglessness. As the brilliant Catholic author of the mid-twentieth century, Flannery O'Connor, once noted, "If you live today, you breathe in nihilism … it's the gas you breathe."

But I don't want to breathe in nihilism and, as a father, I surely don't want my daughters to be poisoned by its vapors. I want them to see the good of creation. I yearn for the infusion of hope, faith, and love into their everyday life to serve as a bulwark against the forces which seek to diminish the soul. My greatest desire is for my daughters to be deeply rooted in their Catholic faith and simultaneously capable of confidently navigating the cultural minefield of the modern world. I would love them to be "in the world, but not of the world." What, then, is a father to do?

There seem to be only two choices.

The first choice is to hunker down as a Church and family, to create a protective bubble and become "smaller and purer." The second choice is to follow Christ's charge to "go and make disciples of all nations." It is a choice between turning inward or going outward. It is an option to consolidate and fortify or to loosen and disseminate. Already, it is easy to envision certain factions that would argue for one approach or the other. So which is it? In choosing a path that will best equip my children to engage the culture they will grow up in and yet not lose their soul, here is what I have concluded: The answer is both.

Smaller and Purer

First, let me describe what is meant by "smaller and purer." This is a phrase that has been attributed to Pope Benedict XVI (as Cardinal Joseph Ratzinger), but may never have been said by him. Instead, in his book-length interview with Peter Seewald, *Salt of the Earth*, Cardinal Ratzinger made the following observation, which may have given rise to the smaller and purer concept:

> Perhaps the time has come to say farewell to the idea of traditionally Catholic cultures. Maybe we are facing a new and different kind of epoch in the Church's history, where Christianity will again be characterized by the mustard seed, where it will exist in small, seemingly insignificant groups that nonetheless live an intensive struggle against evil and bring good into the world—that let God in.[21]

In saying this, Cardinal Ratzinger is not trying to advocate for the formation of a stiff, parochial Catholic enclave. Rather, he laments the disappearance of a more pervasive societal devotion to Catholic values, while simultaneously holding out hope for the Catholic worldview germinating in and emanating from smaller cultural pockets. His larger point is that if you want to be Catholic in the modern world, you must first know what it means to be Catholic. You must start by being smaller and purer.

Before the disciples were empowered by Christ to "go out and make disciples of all nations," this ragtag group of fishermen and tax collectors, doubters and traitors, spent three years learning from the Master. They were small and ever-attempting to be pure. Perhaps we, too, are being called to model ourselves after Jesus' chosen few.

How do we do this?

1. Prayer

2. Living the sacraments

3. Studying the sources of the Catholic faith

Let me elaborate.

PRAYER

We are called to cultivate and model a life of prayer. As St. Padre Pio said, "Pray, hope, and don't worry." In an age of self-sufficiency and instant gratification, the arts of prayer, trust, and discernment have been sorely neglected. If we believe what we say in the Nicene Creed, God is an ever-present, all-powerful Father in love with His creation, longing for dialogue and deeply invested in bringing us into His grace. Whether it is the Lord's Prayer, petitions for specific concerns, "shooting" prayers at random people for their well-being, random snippets of conversation with God, or simply being quiet in the presence of God, prayer connects. It is vital for us to deepen and widen this connection to God and to teach our children how to pray, when to pray, and what to pray about. We can pray in innumerable ways at any time for countless reasons.

Prayer exemplifies to our children that, like all relationships worth cultivating, God deserves our time.

LIVING THE SACRAMENTS

God is present everywhere. Even so, some promote the notion of "thin places": locations where the spiritual distance between heaven and earth seems blessedly thin. Perhaps the most famously visited "thin places" are the lonely peaks of Ireland and the Christ-trodden regions in the Holy Land. These regions provide experiences that are transformative. And yet, a thin distance between God and man requires no travel to far-flung locales. It can be experienced daily in the sacraments of the Church. And the frequency and depth with which we experience the sacraments draw us ever closer to the life-changing grace of God.

Baptism, the Eucharist, reconciliation, confirmation, marriage, holy orders, and the anointing of the sick crystallize the daily "thin places" that cleanse, educate, appoint, collect, and heal us. By frequently bringing our children into the presence of the sacraments and explaining to them why the sacraments matter, we encourage them to return to these "thin places" again and again for solace and sustenance. The sacraments make great demands of us to improve and, by doing so, humanize us. If we sense and experience this, we will live fuller, richer lives. And so will our children.

Studying the Sources
of the Catholic Faith

For the last several years, I have enjoyed teaching recently confirmed high school students who are seeking continued faith formation. In one particular discussion, I bring in over one hundred books and create a series of concentric circles displaying the sources of the Catholic faith. The greatest sources of the Faith reside at the center and are progressively supported by the widening concentric circles of lesser works around them.

The circles begin with the invisible Holy Spirit and the visible Gospels, and emanate outward toward the great apologists of Church history, culminating in what I have named, "Echoes of God in a Secular World." These are encounters with the beauty of God, such as the works of da Vinci, Michelangelo, Mozart, Bernini and others, which the prevailing culture may not recognize as such.

As the students gaze upon the enormity of sources and find themselves moving from the innermost ring to the outermost, they are challenged to consider the vast riches of faith before them. These books are only a small sample of Catholicism's immense resources. Once they have contemplated what is before them, I direct them to return their attention to the center of the concentric circles and then ask, "How many of you have read one complete Gospel?" A few hands go up, but otherwise, there is silence. I then inquire, "Then how can you reason that you have fully explored your faith?" In a world that has given up on faith before even trying, I am often reminded of my favorite quote from G. K. Chesterton: "The Christian ideal has not been tried and found wanting; it has been found difficult and left untried."

How does studying the sources of the Faith help us in our role as Catholics and as parents? We provide our children a model of earnestness for deeper understanding. We are more capable of guiding our children's spiritual reading. And most importantly, we become more fluent with the truths of the Faith in order to better answer our children's questions.

But what about Christ's mandate that we are to "go and make disciples of all nations"? Have we just withdrawn, fortified ourselves, and left the culture to fend for itself? Absolutely not. After we have spent time being "smaller and purer"—after immersing ourselves in prayer, in the sacraments, and in the sources—we find ourselves edified for the next part of our journey. We are in a stronger and more faith-filled position to engage a culture of nihilism. As such, we are better equipped to guide our children. We are richer for having spent time in the presence of Christ, but Christ bids us to go out into the world.

Go and Make Disciples of All Nations

After the Resurrection, the disciples gathered in a place where Jesus soon appeared to them.

> When they saw him, they worshiped, but they doubted. Then Jesus approached and said to them, "All pow-

er in heaven and on earth has been given to me. Go, therefore, and make disciples of all nations, baptizing them in the name of the Father, and of the Son, and of the Holy Spirit, teaching them to observe all that I have commanded you. And behold, I am with you always, until the end of the age." (Matthew 28:17-20, NAB)

Even after spending time with Jesus Christ, witnessing His miracles, hearing His incomparable wisdom and encountering Him after the Resurrection, the disciples still doubted. And once again, Christ reassured them. *Here is your call. Now, go. You are not alone.*

Thus, as Christ's followers were called to make disciples of all nations, we are first parents called to make disciples of our children as they enter deeper into the modern, unbelieving culture. What further message can we give to them and others to sustain and grow their faith?

PRAYER, AGAIN

It should come as little surprise that the first step in fortifying ourselves and our children for engagement in the larger culture is the same as that which strengthened us in our "smaller and purer" formation. The distractions, temptations, and discouragements we are faced with make the need for prayer even more vital. Pope Benedict XVI articulated this well when he said:

There is not only a physical deafness which largely cuts people off from social life; there is also a "hardness of hearing" where God is concerned, and this is something from which we particularly suffer in our own time. Put simply, we are no longer able to hear God—there are too many different frequencies filling our ears.[22]

The self-sufficient attitude that pervades our culture seeks to convince us that personal and social transformation can only occur via political movements or "self-actualization." In fact, when the disciples failed to exorcise a demon from a young boy, Jesus cast the demon out and then explained the reason for their failure. It wasn't a ten-point political platform or a voyage of self-discovery they required. They needed prayer, faith, and fasting. In a culture of immense spiritual emptiness, we are called to pray without ceasing. It is incumbent on us to ask, seek, and knock for the sake of our family and our society.

CULTIVATING THE MORAL IMAGINATION

Modern culture has a shifting narrative of what is right, what is wrong, or even if there is an acceptable notion of right and wrong. This narrative is informed by little more than the fashionable, the profitable, and the expedient. Confusion reigns where morality is rudderless. That is why it is essential to cultivate our children's moral imagination.

But just what is the moral imagination? It is an imagination enriched by stories and tales rooted in the dignity of man, the call to virtue, the clarity of good and evil, and the constancy of grace. It is the visceral experience of truth as opposed to its cool memorization. Flannery O'Connor crystallized the difference between sterile theory and imaginative experience when she said, "Our response to life is different if we have been taught only a definition of faith than if we have trembled with Abraham as he held a knife over Isaac."

While the concept of moral imagination can seem like a highbrow foray into philosophy and theology, it is easily found in the simplest of Grimm's fairy tales or the most complex of Shakespeare's tragedies. The moral imagination is best nourished with a child in your lap, a book in your hands, and a magical tale on your lips.

Chesterton brilliantly described the essential point—that housed within the wonder of the fairy tale is a burning, uncompromising truth. Children, above all, have a sense of justice, of what is right and wrong, even in the most fantastic of tales. In fact, our children accept all forms of magic and mishap in these stories without question, but trifle with the truth of good and evil and they will accuse us of foul play.

For a modern example, let us consider the *Star Wars* series. Over the course of six movies, we encounter the strangest of creatures, the wildest of technology, and the most foreign of planets. An entire lexicon is created with terms like Jedi and Sith, Wampa and Jawa, Millennium Falcon and Tie Fighter having become common and accepted parlance among the youngest and oldest of fans. And yet all of this incredible unreality is embraced simply because the main narrative centers on the very human experience of a man and his son: Anakin and Luke. Separated by time, place, and experience, this father and son find themselves on trajectories that will soon collide.

And yet it is not back flips and light-saber duels that are ultimately compelling about this man and his boy. It is the fact that each possesses an ineradicable value, or dignity, that is not snuffed out by evil aspirations or humble beginnings. Each feels driven to serve a cause greater than himself. Each is willing to undergo suffering in part because something in their relationship as father and son is deeply amiss and must be rectified. And, finally, each is desperate to give, but also to receive, that final act of grace that impossibly, miraculously turns everything aright.

You see, that's the wondrous thing about *Star Wars*: it's not the exotic that attracts us most. But what attracts instead is the common—the human—that we all have in us. It is the human thirst for value, for hope, and for deliverance. So whether it is *Star Wars*, *Cinderella*, or *The Lego Movie*, the settings change, but the truths are unbending. And our children know it.

When the alternative cultural narrative of meaninglessness and selfishness serves to degrade dignity, purpose, and hope, cultivation of the moral imagination provides a bulwark that is indispensable. Again, Chesterton best explained why: "Fairy tales do not give the child his first idea of [the bogeyman]. What fairy tales give the child is his first clear idea of the possible defeat of [the bogeyman]."

SEEKING TRUTH, GOODNESS, AND BEAUTY IN EVERYTHING

The world and its culture are filled with horrible things. Natural disasters, incurable diseases, ruthless governments, mean-spirited people, mosquitoes. It's easy to be consumed by all the negatives and find ourselves dragged down into depression and despair. And yet, that is not what we are called to do. The young Anne Frank, living under harrowing circumstances while hiding from the Nazis, understood this: "I don't think of all the misery, but of the beauty that still remains." And St. Paul counseled:

> Finally, brothers, whatever is true, whatever is honorable, whatever is just, whatever is pure, whatever is lovely, whatever is gracious, if there is any excellence and if there is anything worthy of praise, think about these things. Keep on doing what you have learned and received and heard and seen in me. Then the God of peace will be with you. (Philippians 4:8-9, NAB)

To find that which is ennobling, it is vital that we know what we are looking for. To see truth, goodness, and beauty, we first need to know what it is. Where, then, do we start looking? I would reason that we should start with the "Echoes of God in a Secular World." This is found in, to name a few, the art of Leonardo da Vinci, Michelangelo and Caravaggio, the architecture of Bernini and Bramante, the music of

Mozart, Haydn and Palestrina, the literature of Dostoyevsky, Shakespeare, and Waugh. The craft of these artists epitomize beauty. And where beauty is, the recognition of goodness and truth soon follow.

But what about our children? Surely, we aren't expecting them to read Shakespeare and listen to classical music (at least not yet). But we could simply go online and show them a picture of the Sistine Chapel, play them an abbreviated piece from Mozart, or give them three lines from Shakespeare to chew on. Likewise, we could explore our local church or art museum, or walk through the paths of the local nature park. And as our children grow, the beauty of these bright minds and brilliant works will not be foreign to them. In the meantime, remember that the narratives of countless modern books, plays, movies, and songs are suffused with the story of a hero (a dignified figure who resonates with us) who is called to a greater task, experiences suffering, and ultimately receives grace.

For instance, a few years ago, I found myself watching *Tangled* with my daughters. *Tangled* is a winsome Disney movie loosely based on the fairy tale *Rapunzel*. As we enjoyed the film, my daughters thought they were simply giggling at the antics of a longhaired girl on a wild adventure. But, in fact, what they were experiencing was much more. A young girl born of royalty (imbued with dignity) finds herself trapped in a tower (enduring suffering), haunted by the desire to see the distant kingdom's floating lanterns (an insistent calling) only to find herself liberated from her confines when she discovers her true and noble identity (receiving grace).

143

In the midst of witty banter, harrowing escape scenes, and felicitous musical numbers (which we all *still* sing as a family), my daughters' eyes were seeing something modern, yet beautiful. And in this beauty was housed truth. The producers and writers of stories like *Tangled* would never admit that there is catholicity to this type of narrative, but even so, there it is. Why are these stories continually produced and reliably successful? Because they speak to a narrative that resonates with our soul: dignity, calling, suffering, and grace. This is the story of Christ. And it is a story of His disciples.

Now, are there plenty of good stories, art, and music spoiled or tainted by sin and error? Absolutely. Should we then dismiss them out of hand? Some, perhaps. But like St. Basil's discerning bumblebees lighting from flower to flower, we can—we must—take what befits us and pass over the rest.

My two daughters are now four and seven. And, if it is possible, I love them more than when I first met them. As they grow older they see more, they hear more, and they experience more. This makes me worry. But it also makes me smile. Why? Because God created them, and He made this world. And He called it "good." Is there tireless work to be done to prepare them for the culture they are now encountering? Absolutely. Can I protect them from every test and challenge they will face? No. But if I simply teach them, model for them, and walk with them in prayer, in their experience of the sacraments, and in their understanding the sources of the Catholic faith, I will give them the best "small and pure" foundation possible.

And if I continue in prayer, endeavor to cultivate their moral imagination, and show them the truth, goodness, and beauty that our culture has to offer, it will best equip them to be Christ's followers answering the call to "go and make disciples of all nations."

The culture we are called to engage is waiting for us. But so is God. We are called to do great things for a wondrous creation. It is up to us to answer faithfully.

* * *

TOD WORNER is married and the father of two young daughters. When he isn't giving piggyback rides, painting little girls' fingernails, and reading fairy tales, he practices internal medicine and writes as "A Catholic Thinker" for Patheos. He converted to Catholicism in 2010.

Cracking the Code

By Brandon McGinley

It's a refrain heard echoing across bars, golf courses, hardware stores—anywhere men gather: "I have no idea what women want." This complaint has provided fodder for sitcoms and films for as long as pictures have moved. At this point, I'd go so far as to say that the voodoo mysteriousness of femininity is more a pop culture trope than a lived reality—that is, Hollywood tells us women are more enigmatic than they actually are.

But pop culture tropes burrow into our psyche nevertheless. We are trained to throw up our hands at the merest inconsistency, the slightest unreasonableness. This is, however, a dangerous habit.

The first problem with the question "What do women want?" is in the number of that noun. It's plural. It lumps all women into an undifferentiated mass. This is the opposite of how we ought to think of our wives. The proper question is: "What does *my wife* want from *me*?" The idea that our wives are nothing more than representatives of an exotic race allows us to keep them at arm's length; it is an excuse to avoid the broad and deep intimacy marriage demands.

Now, placing the question in the singular doesn't totally solve the problem. We're still left with trying to discern an answer that can often seem hazy and elusive.

I've found that the best first step to understanding my wife's needs and desires is to operate under the assumption that she is a human being. That is to say, I assume that she and I are far more the same than we are different. We long for affection, stability, leisure, happiness, love, and, ultimately, what we were made for: eternal communion with God. They're not so mysterious when you think of them like that.

But don't take my word for it. I spoke with two excellent Catholic women who are also writers about what their husbands do to make their families work. Bonnie Engstrom is a blogger and speaker known for her website *A Knotted Life* and for the survival of her stillborn son James, whose story is part of the cause for the canonization of the Venerable Fulton Sheen. Karen Edmisten is an author and blogger who has written or contributed to several Catholic volumes, including *Deathbed Conversions: Finding Faith at the Finish Line*, and *The Rosary: Keeping Company with Jesus and Mary*.

What I learned is what should be obvious to us, provided we listen to our own experience rather than to the self-assured theoreticians of masculinity: There is no one way to be a great husband to your wife, but there are consistent threads that run through successful marriages. We'll consider your role from her perspective in three areas: everyday life, when times are tough, and the domestic church.

DIFFERENT HUSBANDS, SIMILAR LESSONS

I was a little nervous after I spoke with Bonnie. She describes her husband, Travis, as a "guy who can do just about anything" around the house: fix a faulty lawnmower, wire the house for electricity, work with wood for … whatever the house needs wood for, and so on. (Are there any Travises that aren't handy? It seems like a name that destines a boy to be competent with power tools.) I, on the other hand, fear losing my foot to a mower, my nervous system to trillions of electrons, and my fingers to a power saw.

I exaggerate (a little bit). The point is that this particular mark of traditional masculinity does not suit me terribly well. I'm happy to learn what I need to learn to keep the house from falling down, but in the end I'd rather wrangle with a challenging essay than a challenging clog. But one can't help but wonder after listening to a wife praise her handyman husband if, perhaps, lacking this interest makes one seriously deficient.

What a relief it was, then, to listen to Karen relay an image from her experience: it's just as common as not in the Edmisten house for her to be building a bookcase while her husband, Tom, stops by for advice on which tomatoes to use for dinner. This is not, as some Catholic gender-whisperers might suggest, abnormal, unnatural, or any such thing. Karen is not filled with bitterness over this state of affairs. Rather, both she and her husband bring their talents and interests to the marriage, and use them for the good of the marriage.

This is the key point, as Karen put it to me: "Everything [Tom] does is ordered to the good of the family." And Bonnie, without prompting, expressed precisely the same sentiment. They don't expect their husbands to fulfill a role that has been laid out for them by the surrounding culture, old or new. They expect neither Hugh Beaumont from *Leave It to Beaver* nor Sir Lancelot from the twelfth century. They expect, simply, the man each married to be the best version of himself, applying his interests and talents (and perhaps acquiring new ones), always for the good of the family.

But what about when everyday life is supplanted by moments of deep heartache? In her book *After Miscarriage: A Catholic Woman's Companion to Healing and Hope*, Karen wrote about her experience of losing five unborn children, and she spoke to me about Tom's role in coping with the loss. He fulfilled the typical manly role as a bastion of emotional strength for her, but, importantly, he "didn't feel that he had to be strong for [her] 100 percent of the time." Tom was "every bit as sad" as Karen, and expressed that, which she appreciated.

This is its own kind of strength—the strength to become vulnerable and to share in grief. Karen relates a brief but poignant anecdote. Back when it seemed they would never be able to have children, she recalls visiting friends who had a precocious toddler ambling here and there across the house. In the car on the way home, Tom said it just broke his heart. It was a simple moment, but the type of emotional sharing that, clearly, makes an impact.

Bonnie remembers when her son, James, was stillborn. Travis calmly leapt into action and reached for holy water to baptize their little boy. Throughout the vigil at the hospital, as James regained and clung to life, Travis would get up extra early in the morning in order to visit with his newborn son without losing time with the rest of the kids. At the same time, while others were planning James's funeral, Travis helped organize a prayer vigil, at which he announced to more than one hundred people that "James is gonna be fine." And so he was.

This is just another example of strength: faithful, hope-filled practicality. As Bonnie put it, Travis "knew what to do" and executed it, most importantly in the most extreme moments.

Again, we see different examples of the same concept appreciated by wives: strength in tragedy. How that strength manifests itself will differ from man to man, from marriage to marriage, but it is authentic mental and emotional strength that is valued.

It is perverse that we associate with masculinity the sacrificial strength described above, but also spiritual aloofness.

The upkeep of the domestic church is culturally associated with mom far more than dad. This is a topic that has been discussed by many men throughout this book, so not much more needs to be said here. One example, though, shows how even the little things dads do that we hardly notice ourselves are appreciated not just by the kids, but by mom as well.

Karen told me that Tom, like most men, would say she's done most of the work raising the kids in the Faith. Even so, he has established little traditions, such as telling the kids about the week's Gospel reading on the way to Mass and rounding up the kids for nighttime prayer, that ensure that he is seen as actively involved in the spiritual life of the family.

Affective displays of spirituality may not be your thing. I know that I prefer the spiritual exercises I perform generally to be private. There are many ways, though, to be a witness to faithfulness that fit within one's preferred spiritual disciplines. Being that witness not only complements our wives' efforts in forming faithful children, but ensures that we are working together as a team to raise our children in the faith.

THE ROLE OF PROVIDER, EXPANDED

In my discussions with Bonnie and Karen, one insight, shared by both, rose to the top: they love that their husbands are committed to providing better lives for their families. Now, we usually associate the role of provider exclusively with financial stability. *The* role of the father, we're told, is to provide material security for the family.

That traditional concept, though, only tells part of the story. "Providing a better life" goes well beyond paychecks. Sometimes it includes home repairs; other times, freshly prepared meals. Sometimes it includes maintaining a stoic countenance through emotional turmoil; other times it means deploying emotional intelligence to empathize or to console. Sometimes it includes leading the family in prayer; other times it includes praying for the family in solitude.

Different men will use different gifts and different skills to provide for their families in different ways. We, like women, are individual human beings; our excellence, except inasmuch as it is shared in pursuing holiness, is not uniform. We are not representatives of a type.

So, no, there is no foolproof answer even to the better question: "What does *my wife* want from *me*?" But I am willing to hazard a guess: If you apply your talents, your skills, and your vocation consistently and joyfully to providing for the best life for your family—comprehensively in this world and the next—then you should be on the right track.

Endnotes

[1] *Puebla: A Pilgrimage of Faith* (Boston: Daughters of St. Paul, 1979), 86.

[2] http://www.covenanteyes.com/pornstats/, accessed September 18, 2014.

[3] http://www.familysafemedia.com/pornography_statistics.html, accessed September 18, 2014.

[4] Ibid.

[5] Ibid.

[6] Ibid.

[7] Ibid.

[8] Russell Scott Smith, "Porn Reborn—From TV to Books to Movies, Sex Still Sells," *New York Post*, September 25, 2003.

[9] *The Social Costs of Pornography* (Princeton, NJ: The Witherspoon Institute, 2005), 38.

[10] H. Rupp and K. Wallen, "Sex Differences in Response to Visual Sexual Stimuli: A Review," *Archives of Sexual Behavior*, April 2008, vol. 37.

[11] William M. Struthers, *Wired for Intimacy: How Pornography Hijacks the Male Brain* (Downers Grove, IL: InterVarsity Press, 2009). See chap. 4, "Your Brain on Porn," for a detailed discussion of brain science and pornography.

[12] Laurie Heap, M.D., "Is Staying in Love Possible … Not Broken, Just Bent," ruhealthyruhappymd.com, April 29, 2013.

[13] Patrick J. Carnes, Ph.D., *Out of the Shadows, Understanding Sexual Addiction* (Center City, MN: Hazelden, 2001), chap. 1.

[14] Ted Roberts, *Pure Desire: How One Man's Triumph Can Help Others Break Free from Sexual Temptation* (Ada, MI: Bethany House, 2008), chap. 3.

[15] Rod Handley, *Character Counts: Who's Counting Yours?* (Grand Island, NE: Cross Training Publishing, 2002), 48-49.

[16] Jeanna Bryner, "Close Friends Less Common Today," www.livescience.com, reporting on a study by Matthew E.

Brashears (2011): "Small Networks and High Isolation? A Reexamination of American Discussion Networks," *Social Networks*, 33(4): 331-341.

[17] S. E. Taylor, L. C. Klein, B. P. Lewis, T. L. Gruenewald, R. A. R. Gurung, & J. A. Updegraff. "Behavioral Responses to Stress: Tend and Befriend, Not Fight or Flight," *Psychological Review*, 107.

[18] Anthony Percy, *The Theology of the Body Made Simple* (Boston: Pauline, 2006) is a good place to start for those unfamiliar with this series of teachings.

[19] Peter Kleponis, *The Pornography Epidemic: A Catholic Approach* (Oldsmar, FL: Women of Grace, 2012).

[20] Adapted from Jay Dennis, *Our Hardcore Battle Plan: Joining in the War Against Pornography* (Birmingham, AL: New Hope, 2013).

[21] Peter Seewald, *Salt of the Earth* (San Francisco: Ignatius, 2013), 16.

[22] Pope Benedict XVI, Homily, Munich, Germany, September 10, 2006.

The Editor

BRANDON MCGINLEY writes from his hometown of Pittsburgh, Pennsylvania, where he lives with his wife, Katie, and their young daughter, Teresa. They excitedly await an addition to the family around the time this book is published. By day, Brandon works for the Pennsylvania Family Institute, a nonprofit public policy organization. By night, he writes, tries his hand at mixing cocktails, then writes some more. His work has appeared in print in *National Review*, *Fare Forward*, and the *Pittsburgh Catholic*; and online at *First Things*, *The Federalist*, *Public Discourse*, and *Acculturated*.